THE SABBATICAL METHOD

How to Leverage Rest and Grow Your Business

ALYSON CAFFREY

BIG PRINT
p u b l i s h i n g

Big Print Publishing

www.BigPrintPublishing.com

The Sabbatical Method © Copyright 2023 Alyson Caffrey

First Edition

Published in the United States by Big Print Publishing

Big Print Publishing | www.bigprintpublishing.com

An imprint of Dinosaur House

For more information, email hello@operationsagency.com.

ISBN: 978-1-961462-99-1 (hardcover)
        978-1-961462-98-4 (paperback)
        978-1-961462-97-7 (ebook)

Praise for the Sabbatical Method

As a seasoned entrepreneur with over 20 years of experience, I can attest to the fact that building a successful business is not a sprint— it's a marathon. And just like any long-distance race, you need to pace yourself if you want to finish strong. The Sabbatical Method is a useful, systematic approach for entrepreneurs who are looking to build a business that will last. By taking a step back and prioritizing rest and delegation, you can create a sustainable business model that will not only benefit you, but your entire team.

—Yuri Elkaim, CEO of Healthpreneur®,
NYT Bestselling Author

Processes and operations are often not considered the sexy part of the business. But is there anything sexier in business than walking away from your computer knowing that everything is taken care of, being able to sleep soundly at night, being stress-free, and spending quality time with the people you love?

Today, that is the most essential part of my business. Systematic operations allow your business to scale and will enable you to have freedom. Alyson is a goldmine of knowledge and experience in setting up a business to function like a well-oiled machine. Be sure to read and implement what she teaches; it WILL change your life.

—Robert Patin, CEO of Creative Agency Success

While working so hard to "succeed," many of us slowly give away our power. We put taking care of ourselves on the back burner. We think, "When I accomplish _____, I will start making my priorities actual priorities." But there is always more that gets put on our to-do lists.

In order to be truly Successful, we must find a way to optimize our health, build incredible relationships and spend quality time with those we love, and have systems in place that make it possible for our businesses to thrive and grow. True Success means thriving in ALL areas of our lives.

How can you design your life to achieve True Success? Start here, with "The Sabbatical Method." Alyson's method will provide you with clear actions to take to start building your business in a way that will support your desire to live a truly successful life, without sacrificing your health, your relationships, or your happiness.

—Emily Dietrich MD, FACOG, Certified High-Performance Coach, Founder of The Doc Box for Female Physicians, Co-Founder of Absolute Athlete Development

I first reached out to Alyson when my less-than-one-year-old business was consuming every waking minute. My wife booked a much-needed vacation for us and our 3 boys, but I was terrified to walk away for a week. Alyson helped me find structure, peace, and calm in my business in a matter of weeks, which allowed us to have an unforgettable family trip. Her methods are solid, proven, and needed for every business owner. Ignore the advice of this book at your own peril.

—Cody Burch, Founder and President of Red Anchor Marketing

Many founders fall into the trap of brute force effort. That works in the early days, maybe. That won't work in the long term, guaranteed. It'll wreck your business and your health. If you're looking to avoid that trap, or get out of it if you've already fallen in, then look no further than "The Sabbatical Method." It's a lifesaver that you'll reference again and again.

—Matt Gartland, Co-founder and CEO of SPI Media

Entrepreneurship is hard. It can drain our time, finances, family, and friends if we don't slow down and set up our businesses properly. "The Sabbatical Method" is the go-to resource for business owners to learn how to structure their business for freedom and impact without losing everything they fought to build.

—Mike Ruman, Founder of Local Growth

Grab Your Toolkit

To get the best experience with this book, I've found readers who download and use The Sabbatical Method™ Toolkit are able to implement faster and take the next steps needed to thrive in just 90 days.

You can get yours by visiting:

www.thesabbaticalmethod.com

This book is for the families of entrepreneurs.

"The music is not in the notes, but in the silence in between." - Mozart

Sab·bat·i·cal

noun

1. A period of paid leave for study or travel
2. A break or change from a normal routine

Meth·od

noun

1. A particular form of procedure for accomplishing something, especially a systematic or established one
2. Orderliness of thought or behavior; systematic planning or action

TABLE OF CONTENTS

A FEW THINGS YOU SHOULD KNOW

Definitions

These are terms I use throughout the book, so you should probably be familiar with them:

- **Mission Critical:** I'm the spouse of a former military man. So, in our house, we say "mission critical" to mean we're discussing something of high importance. I love how simply and elegantly this term illustrates that you cannot ignore {the thing}, or people will die.
- **SOP:** Standard Operating Procedure
- **Elegant:** I say this often, probably because I'm not.
- **Operations, Simplified™:** My core operational framework for assessing the overall health of a business.
- **Mission:** Each chapter will include a mission that is the theme or outcome of the chapter. I include this recuring section to ensure we're on the same page.
- **Summary:** Each chapter will have a summary of significant concepts, key takeaways, and the most important notes.
- **Critical Action:** Each chapter will have a Critical Action. This is an exercise or an action to complete to improve the operational health of your business or clarify where you may be within that process.

Toolkit

I've created a free, online toolkit to lead you through the Sabbatical Method in depth. It holds all the practical exercises, templates, trainings, and tactics I explain in this book. You can get it at thesabbaticalmethod.com/toolkit.

Cheat Sheet

Get the high-level daily habits and weekly activities cheat sheet at thesabbaticalmethod.com/toolkit.

INTRODUCTION

In the summer of 2022, I was approached by a prospective client. We'll call her Miranda. Miranda and her husband had been running a successful coaching business for corporate professionals for years. Her skillset is incredible. She works with high-performing corporate professionals to hone their leadership and transform their working style so they can lead more team members more effectively. Further, particularly for those at high-growth companies, she helps these professionals develop an internal process for developing other new leaders throughout the organization. She's coached clients at tech companies such as Go-Daddy, Airtable, and LinkedIn.

A friend and colleague who knew Mirada well enough to see that she needed support referred her to me. She and I scheduled our first coaching session, and I could honestly tell she was exhausted. Not only by business, but by life. She'd been burning the candle at both ends: coaching clients, being a mom and a spouse, and doing everything full throttle. It was costing her. Her health was in decline, and she felt stuck.

Miranda had also been diagnosed with Lymphedema just a few weeks prior. Now, she'd be *forced* to take a sabbatical from the business to pump her lymphatic system every few hours. Her treatments were so debilitating and frequent that she couldn't even do the things she loved—coach her clients and speak on stage. To make matters worse, Miranda struggled to walk. She physically could not support her own body. She was bound to a cart that helped her navigate most of her travel and needed lots of support to move around her own home. Her marriage was also suffering; in an attempt to support her, Miranda's husband had also been burning the midnight oil, taking on all the work Miranda couldn't handle and managing team members with no understanding of or visibility into what they were doing. They both felt stuck and unsure if either of them could even afford to take the time off that Miranda needed to recover.

Miranda's situation isn't an isolated incident, at least not for entrepreneurs. A study at the National Institute of Mental Health shows entrepreneurs are 3 times more likely to experience mental health issues than our employed counterparts.[1] We're sold this idea that if we leap, if we work on our own, we can live life on our terms. If that concept is true, if we are the grantors of our freedom, why do we feel like we're holding ourselves captive at the same time? Why are we subjecting ourselves to all this pain?

Over the last 5 years supporting businesses at Operations Agency, I've seen owners struggle to keep their personal lives from falling apart. They spend so much time reacting to the fires set inside their business that they barely have time to eat healthy nutritious meals. They don't spend any time with their families. They don't move their bodies. It's incredible to me how quickly someone can start a business, and shortly afterward, they're apparently living in a cage, unable to take vacation or even shut their laptop at 6pm.

Here's my message to my fellow business owners:

---

[1] "Mental Illness," National Institute of Mental Health (U.S. Department of Health and Human Services), accessed May 2, 2023, https://www.nimh.nih.gov/health/statistics/mental-illness.

If you keep treating your body like a rental and ignoring your basic needs, you'll end up like Miranda: full of health problems and forced to lay down multiple times per day to pump junk out of your body. And when we treat our businesses this way, we fail. That's why 65 percent of businesses don't make it to the 10-year mark.[2] We're indoctrinated to believe that if we just hustle harder, work longer, spend more, bring in more, *then* we'll finally be successful. But that's like beating your head against a concrete wall over and over again. Sure, breaking through is a *possibility*, but you'll certainly be damaged, whether you break through or not. The reality is, if you create a more sustainable way of operating your business and integrating your life, you will be able to outlast your competition and actually enjoy the ride.

Why Rest?

I'd like you to consider for a moment training for one of the most difficult physical feats known to man: climbing Mount Everest.

Only 800 people per year attempt to make the trek, and an average of about 500 actually make it to base camp. It's a climber's bucket-list item, and many who make it to the top, go back for more. The view is apparently (quite literally) breathtaking, and the technical climbing is peak level. Climbers train for years to summit Everest. The trek itself is 10 weeks in length. Depending on the size of the climbing party, gear, skillset, and weather, it can take as long as 7 weeks to climb through the more challenging parts.

---

[2] Deane, Michael T. "Top 6 Reasons New Businesses Fail." Investopedia. Investopedia, January 2, 2023. https://www.investopedia.com/financial-edge/1010/top-6-reasons-new-businesses-fail.aspx#:~:text=According%20to%20the%20U.S.%20Bureau,to%2015%20years%20or%20more.

A training plan from the popular Alpine Ascents: Mountain Guides lists some of the requirements necessary to be considered physically ready to climb to the roof of the world. They say in their training plan that one must have a baseline of peak physical fitness for at least 6 to 9 months prior to even beginning the one-year long Everest training plan. Climbers must be able to summit 4,000 feet climbs on consecutive days carrying about 50 to 60 pounds.

Cardiovascular training is by far the most highlighted skill, as the oxygen levels at peak points in the Everest climb can cause severe health issues to someone who gets a minor flu. Experts recommend reserving about 6 hours per week for peak cardiovascular training during the year of preparation, and to complete hours at varying levels of elevation.

Among all the skills necessary to climb Everest—cardiovascular, climbing, strength, and flexibility—the common thread for success is rest.

Adequate rest in any high-intensity training plan is critical. During training, muscle tissue is broken down, and the body is challenged in a litany of ways. Rest days allow the muscles to repair themselves and increase their glycogen stores to perform in the next challenge. Studies suggest that about 60 percent of high-performing athletes suffer from overtraining: they literally don't know how to rest. They don't give their body opportunities to recover, which can have severely damaging consequences, such as increased injuries, heart arrhythmia, fatigue, and depression.[3]

---

[3] Elizabeth Quinn, MS. "What Are the Warning Signs of Overtraining Syndrome?" Verywell Fit. Verywell Fit, October 17, 2022. https://www.verywellfit.com/overtraining-syndrome-and-athletes-3119386.

Ian Taylor, who summited Everest in 2008, reports that the most common setback for climbers is not giving themselves enough time to acclimate to the altitude and reduced oxygen levels.[4] He says simple altitude sickness can be damaging to the body and the mind if climbers don't give themselves enough time to acclimate for the next phase of the climb. And in a fight to the world's tallest peak, a little damage to the body, a little less mental health, can be the difference between life, and death.

Reports show that entrepreneurs work an average of 50 hours per week. The most rigorous Everest training plans incorporate between 12 and 24 hours (including rest) of training time per week. So, compared to the ambitious Everest trainee, entrepreneurs are spending *double* the time just working in their businesses, not to mention any time spent on physical training, volunteering, serving on boards, public service, or being primary or secondary caregivers to kids, pets, or elderly parents.

If we want to perform at high levels for extended periods of time, rest is not optional. It's a fundamental piece we must take seriously and weave intentionally into our approach. With proper training and proper rest, we increase longevity, physical ability, and mental health, and become holistically capable of meeting our dreams' demands.

My goal with this book is to help you strategically leverage rest while simultaneously improving your business operations. I call this the Sabbatical Method, which I'll break down in more detail later.

---

[4] ITT_User. "How Many People Have Climbed Mount Everest?" Ian Taylor Trekking, April 25, 2023. https://iantaylortrekking.com/blog/how-many-people-have-climbed-mount-everest/#:~:text=All%20of%20this%20begs%20the,to%20the%20Everest%20Base%20Camp.

I've seen this method offer health back to my clients, bring sanity back to teams, add life into dreams, and allow owners to scale beyond their projections and so much more. I'm convinced that implementing strategic rest and removing yourself from your business is the most impactful and sustainable way to not only stay in business but grow long term. Many founders are forced into rest when they're burnt out or something terrible happens. What if we approached rest proactively instead of waiting for everything to fall apart? What if we could use rest *strategically* to improve the outcomes in our business and create a more sustainable operation?

In 2023 and beyond, it's easier than ever to start working for yourself. The Great Resignation of 2022 and the post-Covid workplace have given more families and more individuals the opportunity to create their own schedules, earn income on their own terms, and create a balance for life and work that is fulfilling. But we've got to find a way to make it work *in the long run.*

The EA (Everything Administrator)

I got started in operations back in 2016. I'd been working for a company for a year, supporting the founder as an executive assistant, and my role quickly evolved… considerably. In the first few months of my employment, we'd hosted a live event, created a new coaching program, and filled it with entrepreneurs looking to sharpen their speaking skills and leverage speaking engagement to gain more clients within their businesses.

I'll never forget being a young and hungry new professional having the opportunity to support these clients. I was fascinated by how they'd taken the leap from employee to self-employed, created a business, and were now sharing their impactful stories with the world.

One of the first deliverables of our coaching program was a one-day intensive. Most clients flew out to our small office in Colorado Springs where we rolled out our gigantic whiteboard and our team took them through the company signature framework for leveraging speaking engagements to grow their businesses. The experience was transformational and confronting. Sitting in these meetings I realized that almost all of the people we worked with were suffering from some kind of fatigue. Non-profit founders, motivational speakers, coaches of varying industries were all getting things very wrong. Their lives seemed so glamorous on the surface, but behind the scenes, these people were drowning. Most had only a handful of employees (if any at all), spent their days on the road going from gig to gig, ran their business haphazardly, and barely spent any time with their families. Many had declining health from eating fast-food and lacking the time and infrastructure to move their bodies. When they showed up to our office, they were incredibly excited and entirely drained, and nothing in most of their businesses was sustainable without their direct input.

As the company I worked for grew, we invited more team members, hosted more events, launched new programs, and created an online course. I was at the operational helm. Our founder was also on the road quite often, speaking and sharing his story about growing a national nonprofit with speaking teams. Most ventures begin this way: a few people, an abundance of skills, late nights, and a figure-it-out mindset. There's no systemization, because, well, you don't even know what you'd systemize yet. You're not only building the airplane while you're flying it, but you're also trying to figure out if you're flying an airplane, piloting a helicopter, or captaining a submarine. We were rolling with the punches and being agile as all hell. The results we achieved for our clients were incredible, but behind the scenes, things seemed to be held together with duct tape. Worse, we had no idea what metrics to use to determine success, where to find specific tools we needed to do our jobs properly, and what tasks should take priority. It led to messy client agreements, requests for refunds, challenges training and keeping team members, lack of reporting, and, ultimately, emotional decision-making. It was taxing on everyone, especially the founder.

I found myself in the chief holding-it-all-together role. I was the head of customer success, doing all the partner contracts, planning our events and our workshops, compiling all the sales and marketing reports, connecting the team with resources, and handling all of our internal projects.

I was what is commonly referred to as a "unicorn" in small-business staffing—someone with loads of skills and their hands in several different—and in my case, large—initiatives in the business. I supported the founder with everything from managing his executive assistant to leading our quarterly strategic planning. I very frequently stepped into the financial controller position creating reports on operational spending and customer acquisition costs, forecasting goals for our sales and events departments, approving final bills from vendors, keeping QuickBooks up-to-date, and processing payroll. It seemed there was nothing that wasn't part of my job description... or at least added to my plate.

Then, my husband and I got a letter in the mail that made things *really* crazy.

My husband and I received a notice from his commanding officer that he had been selected to join the 160th Special Operations Aviation Regiment, nicknamed the Night Stalkers. This was basically the most prestigious level that he could operate at within the Army. Ever seen the movie *Black Hawk Down*? They were the Night Stalkers.

My husband, Steve, had been in the Army for just over 2 years and had recently been named sergeant at an incredibly quick rate. He was DA-selected[5] and informed this new opportunity was in Fort Campbell, Kentucky, and would begin in just 8 weeks. We sat on the couch in our small apartment in Colorado Springs just pondering what to do. We knew this was an incredible opportunity, but it meant things would change substantially for our family. I would need to move home to New Jersey and live with my parents while he completed 3 months of intense training. We'd need to find a new place to live, a new support system, and I'd need to find a new job. We trusted the opportunity in front of us, deciding to move forward. Steve would have to begin training for this elite team in Virginia within 2 months.

I requested a meeting with my boss, and I was anxious. I knew what my departure would mean to the business, to him. Our team was based almost entirely in Colorado Springs, and we had in-person workshops we were putting on between 4 to 6 times per year with plans to add more. Leaving the state while keeping my role would have meant flying back and forth several times per year and spending about a third of my time in Colorado. With Steve gone nearly 50 percent of his time, this just wasn't feasible. Still, at this point, all the business operations were flowing through me.

When I broke the news that I needed to leave, my boss was both shocked and supportive. It took a few long meetings to discuss several details of my departure and decide how we would break things to the team, but ultimately, he asked me for a 3-month transition period. At the time, I thought, *What must it feel*

---

[5] "DA selection" in the US Army is a prestigious selection by your commanding officer to do a specific duty. Lots of folks get "DA-selected" for leadership roles and elite forces if they've been observed by leadership as outstanding in their current role.

like to run your own shop yet depend on someone else to this degree?

Though I was "operations director" in title at the time, I was so much more. When we sat down to create my 90-day transition plan, I found myself taking a tally of all the processes I may need to write down, team trainings I'd need to compile, and reports I'd need to prepare. I scheduled meetings with team members to transfer knowledge. I recorded these sessions so that they could be turned into training documents and referenced after my departure. It was an immense amount of work. And I didn't know it at the time, but it was critical to the company's success. Finally, the teams I'd managed had concrete metrics and processes to point them in the right direction. Templates to help them move faster. Because I had paved the operational path, a new operations director was able to come in, quickly orient themselves, and run things even better than I ever had.

At the end of my 90-day transition, I transferred all my "keys to the kingdom" to my replacement. I remember talking with the founder on the phone on my last official day, and he was so grateful for my work and seemed to have a renewed excitement for the growth of the organization with my replacement.

I didn't realize it then, but I had just revitalized the business. I gave the founder a brand-new foundation on which to build his dream business. Those efforts have seen them through 5 years of incredible growth, which have included partnerships with top-notch speakers such as Grant Cardone and other incredible industry leaders. My input at least partially prepped them for a growth period that helped their business serve millions of people. They'll happily beat the odds and create lasting impact, because they have what lots of other businesses don't have—sustainable operations.

***

My transition time with that organization officially ended in August of 2017. By October of the very same year, I was completely booked with new clients wanting the same support I had given the founder of that organization. My clients had been running things alone or with a handful of team members and they were tired of doing everything on their own. The systems and structure that my team provided became the way my new clients were able to do things like take multi-week vacations with their families, grow businesses to the 8-figure mark without burning out, prepare for profitable exits, grow from 5 to 50 locations, and so much more.

Take Andriea, CEO of Image Care Centers in Hackettstown, New Jersey. She was looking for a frictionless way to expand their footprint in the North Jersey area and keep employee training consistent. When they came on board with Operations Agency in 2020, they had only 4 offices and 50 employees. Now, they have 20+ facilities and over 500 employees. In July of 2022, we helped them open their first medical imaging facility inside of a Jefferson Hospital, giving them a system they can use to open in major hospital systems nationwide. They'll likely be in acquisition territory in the near future.

Then there's Cody, founder and president of Red Anchor Marketing. He came to us back in 2017 with aspirations to simply take a week-long family vacation to Walt Disney World without his entire business falling apart. We installed some simple systems to help with his client fulfillment and overall management. He's been taking consistent vacations with his family while building his business over the last 5 years, all while sitting front-row at all his son's week-day wrestling matches and football games.

I get emails and Facebook messages from folks who tell me implementing my methods helped save their marriage, created more efficiency and ownership among their teams, and bridged disagreements between managing partners. In early 2020, I held an annual planning workshop that focused on input instead of output, and every single attendee, despite a global pandemic that year, later reported to me that they had either met or exceeded the expectations we'd planned together. We've helped plenty of other industry leaders improve their customer experience, creating repeat processes that build trust and consistency.

Overall, my work over the last 5 years running Operations Agency has been dedicated to helping owners have *agency* over their life and their business. To not work in a cage that demands long travel, nights, weekends, and time away from their families.

> At Operations Agency, our mission is to return fulfilled founders back to their families so that they can stay in business and change the world with their solutions.

These pages will help you create the longevity to outlast your competition and create an asset that can function independently of any one person on your team. With these tools, tactics, and strategies, you'll be able to take vacations, plan big goals, grow your family, and become more active in your community. This book is the key to preparing us to be present during the entire path of life, not just referencing photos of the milestones.

It's easier than ever to start a business, but it's harder than ever to keep one. The Bureau of Labor Statistics shows that 20 percent of businesses fail in the first 2 years, 45 percent during the first 5, and 65 percent by the tenth. Layer the "hustle" mindset on top of it, and it's no wonder we have so many entrepreneurs who are burnt out, ignoring their health, divorcing their spouses, or raising kids with mental health issues.

Overdue for Systems

If you had operations in place, you could create a more predictable business, strategize new growth opportunities, get out of the core functions of your business, and actually spend quality time doing the things you love. A balance could exist, between impact and input.

Many owners I work with know they need systems (they may have even read 50 books and articles on the subject). They know they're overdue to create resources for team members, such as templates folks can use in their absence. They know they should let go. I'll bet you do, too. The trouble is getting there.

The good news is, you're holding the key to creating organization, without needing to hit the pause button on all your creativity. In this book, I demystify the process of adding structure to your business. I walk you through a reset that encourages positive change. This method isn't just for owners who want to scale businesses to create empires or prep for 9-figure exits. This is for the owner who runs a small shop and wants to leave for a vacation without the pain of needing to answer client emails. For the mompreneur who is afraid to show her team that she's pregnant. For the team who feels stuck. For the founder who still gets on sales calls and is, deep down, afraid to close because they know what one more client or project could mean for them and their team.

I've been there. I've helped many clients who've been there. And I'm writing this now to help you get out from there. Over the course of this book, we're going to build muscles. And not the ones in your body. We're going to build muscles in your business to help it become strong and independent. I'm going to show you the framework I've used to lay the foundation for every business I've worked with, and we're going to walk this path together. Here. Now.

The Sabbatical Method

I call this the Sabbatical Method. It's a hard reset and a lifestyle change all rolled into one. As owners, we want a business that can function without us. We want to give it that opportunity by taking a step back before we're "volun-told" to.

The Sabbatical Method is both the destination and the journey. Often, I find owners who have put off creating systems and are in need of a hard reset, but that only provides temporary results. They need to optimize the path to success (I'll chat more about this later in Chapter 4) to create a way for them to assess their role in their businesses at a quarterly cadence. As a business grows and evolves, so should the founder's role.

The Sabbatical Method is a totally new way of thinking that will allow you to run your business so that you *can* take full-on sabbaticals where you totally detach from your business. Sound like a pipe dream? It's not—it's fully possible, even if, right now, you'd be happy to get a weekend away from your business.

Sabbaticals of that nature—which I'll call "traditional" sabbaticals—allow you to rethink and reshape your business. With a sabbatical, leaders are able to come back to work refreshed, and ready to move into the next phase of their business.

In the corporate world, in academia, and in many religious organizations, leaders are told to take sabbaticals, where they consummately detach from their everyday work, spend time with their families, travel, and reconnect with spirituality and nature.

These detachments fuel their creativity so when they return, they're far more productive and, more often than not, during the sabbaticals, they have several "aha!" moments that allow them to see where they and/or their team could stop harmful processes, upgrade their models, products, and services, and start new projects that dramatically move the needle. It's no wonder that organizations highly encourage leaders to take sabbaticals. Or force them to.

That's a piece of what I'm saying. Follow the guidance in this book, and one day, you'll be able to take such a sabbatical. But I'm also talking about a regular cadence of detachment from your work.

Rest isn't something we save up for a vacation. Nor is it something we only do once a day. Rest itself pops up in an ongoing cadence on a daily routine—we sleep (hopefully) every 24 hours. Then, most of us try to take 1 to 2 days off a week (even if we aren't currently getting it!). Then, optimally, we all have a 3- or 4- day weekend every quarter or so, and maybe every year we take a couple weeks off and travel with family.

Rest wouldn't work in only one way or the other—obviously, we can't survive without daily sleep, and, even if we did have daily sleep, we'd be living a fairly mundane and boring life without our holidays, romantic getaways, travels, and vacations, and our (again, hopefully) weekly breaks from work.

All of these times—that are supposed to be detachments from our work—allow us to live a fully productive life.

What I'm going to teach you will afford you the opportunity to add these cadences into your life. Importantly, entrepreneurs and founders, especially, need micro-doses of detachment from our ongoing daily struggles. We are fighters and warriors. And when we skip out on these micro detachments, we lose our way, and slowly but surely, we pile on slightly worse and worse decisions—we don't train our staff, we let poor processes become commonplace, and we fail to streamline activities. In the end, costs rise, profits fall, and our time erodes. Then, we simply *can't* take a traditional sabbatical: *How on Earth could I leave for a month, or even a weekend, when my business is hanging by a thread?* many founders eventually start to think.

But believe it or not, if you follow the steps in this book, you'll begin to find areas where you can detach, slowly but surely, trusting others and allowing *processes* to create predictable outcomes that don't fully depend on you. With some of these micro-doses of mental breaks, you'll begin to make better and better decisions. Eventually, you *will* be able to take regular, full-on breaks from your work.

Many of us commonly refer to our businesses as our "baby," and if you're a parent reading this, you understand that responsibility: sleepless nights, constant attention, no time for yourself, no other personal relationships. Everything stops in service of keeping this new, little, fragile life alive.

But then, the baby gets older. He learns how to use the bathroom, tie his shoes, and brush his teeth. He may even begin to help with chores, change his bed sheets, and wipe down the counter.

Our ultimate goal as parents is to raise a baby into capable adolescence and then, eventually, into adulthood with total autonomy. Why don't we take that same approach with our businesses?

Businesses remain our babies for too long. And then we grow to resent the amount of attention they need over time. Imagine needing to go to kindergarten with your son or daughter to change their diaper or watch them eat lunch in fear of them choking on their peanut butter and jelly sandwich. It sounds ridiculous, but many do this with their businesses.

If you're finding that you're struggling to take an afternoon, a weekend, or a full week to step out of the business and let your systems do the managing, hold tight, because we're going to change that. Within a 90-day timeframe, we want to assess where your business operations currently are, and craft some Critical Actions you can take to add some structure, which will eventually allow you more time off.

So many solutions like the Entrepreneurial Operating System (EOS) get things wrong. It shouldn't take a year for your business to mature to the level of self-sustainment. Over the next 90 days, if you implement the Critical Actions at the end of each chapter, you will see a business that is more self-sustaining and more complimentary to your life. I'll walk you through my Operations, Simplified™ framework to assess where your operations are now, and then, I'll equip you with the practical tools to implement systems and processes into each of the core operational levels of a business. The beauty of this method is that you can use it again, each quarter, to actualize the business you want to run and the life you want to live.

Throughout this journey together, I'll highlight key findings and examples from businesses I've actually worked with, my own experience growing and managing my own company, as well as industry examples of founders who have taken extremely impactful sabbaticals.

We can no longer expect to feed our business junk and have it running properly. We wouldn't do that to our bodies or to our minds, and we can't treat our businesses that way. No more shooting from the hip, no more reacting to daily fires with no balance. No more sleepless nights or micromanaging every single step of others' work.

A Few Requirements

Before we dive in, let me tell you who this won't work for:

This won't work for someone who can't take ownership of their actions or who can't keep their word.

The simplest way you can begin to build the life and business of your dreams is to do what you say you're going to do. Period. Apply it to your clients, to your team, to your partners. And, hey, if you struggle keeping your commitments, here's your permission to make less of them.

This won't work for the person who needs everything to be perfect.

I used to be in this camp, too. It doesn't serve. You won't help your customers if you keep your solutions to yourself. Imagine the impact you can make on families, communities, and other organizations doing powerful things. Done is better than perfect. Just get it done and improve from there.

This won't work for anyone who makes excuses.

Listen, people deserve grace. I wholeheartedly believe that. But have you ever been in touch with someone who's just making it work despite the odds? And you wonder, *How do they do it all?* This is why: They don't make excuses. They just do the thing. There's a famous Teddy Roosevelt quote that goes, "The credit belongs to the [wo]man who is actually in the arena," but no one finishes the line very often. He also goes on to say: "whose face is marred with dust and sweat and blood." Running a business is tough shit. And most fail. If you're going to make excuses about why you can't create structure, you'll fail and someone else will rise to take your place.

If you're still with me, good. We have some work to do.

Like anything in life worth achieving, this journey is going to challenge you at times. I've set up this book to give you the tools you need to succeed, but it's no substitute for hard work.

It's impossible to make guarantees on outcomes. I will say this: every client I've worked with, every workshop I've led, and every team I've directly impacted, has been in better health as a company from implementing just one of the functions of my framework.

Operations aren't sexy. I'll say it point blank. But the results sure are.

This is the stuff that keeps us in business. The tried and tested and successful practices that the businesses who are around 10, 15, and 20 years after founding have implemented, iterated on, and continue to build because they know it works. And operations are exactly the first step to true rest.

If you want to make an impact, build a legacy, or prepare a valuable, sellable asset, building systems so you can rest is mission critical.

The information space is flooded with information on how to start your own business, generate an idea, quit your job, and work for yourself. That's all great. You won't get very far in entrepreneurship if you don't know how to bet on yourself. But we need to also begin sharing (louder for the people in the back!) that running a business doesn't have to be a race to the bottom with only a 3-percent success rate.

Let's be change agents. Let's make sure your business stays in business and goes on to serve millions in the future. I'm here to guide you through the process and I hope you're ready for the transformation.

In a time where it's easy to be average, let's be more.

Yours operationally

CHAPTER 1

OPERATIONS = OUTCOMES

Mission: Create clear systems and an operational structure for your business to gain agency over your life. As Uncle Ben says in *Spiderman.* "With great power, comes great responsibility."

On a balmy evening on June 7, 2018, Anthony Bourdain missed dinner. He was in France filming with *CNN* for his newly released series, *Parts Unknown.*

His career was filled with accolades, experiences, fortune, fame, and writings that many up-and-coming chefs and at-home cooks admired.

One of the reasons folks loved Anthony Bourdain was because he was open, honest, and blunt about pretty much everything he did. He was openly critical of his industry, exposing a behind-the-scenes look at restaurants in his memoir *Kitchen Confidential* in 2000. His eats were incredible, but it was his words that made him famous and admired.

Life was an adventure for Bourdain. Viewers of his shows, readers of his books, and his followers felt like they knew him.

He was forthcoming about his drug use, his depression, and his disdain for the public eye.

But missing dinner... was unusual.

That evening Anthony Bourdain hung himself with the belt of a hotel bathrobe. He was 61.

The specifics of his death and the circumstances around it are somewhat unknown, as even the police report filed by the lead investigator does not determine the cause of death. Even the toxicology report read that there were no narcotics in his system—something that Bourdain had been vocal about struggling with in his years as an up-and-coming chef in New York City.

After his death, many close family members and friends spoke about his life and his mental state. Many confirmed that he'd struggled with substances and depression, openly talked about death, and was seeing a psychotherapist for several different issues.

A unifying thread in the interviews about Bourdain, though, wasn't his struggle with depression, his history of drug abuse, or any other mental health highlights. That was just a layer of how those close to him were trying to rationalize his death.

Interestingly, most highlighted "Tony's" work ethic and drive.

In an interview with the *New Yorker*, Morgan Neville, producer of the Anthony Bourdain documentary *Roadrunner*, said, "The reason he kept moving was just the hope that the next thing was going to make him happy, or it was going to solve something in his life. That sense of momentum, it's both part of what made him great, and part of what must have been so tough to live with."

Bourdain's biography on the website of the Culinary Institute of America or "CIA" (where he graduated in 1978), notes that he worked at notable restaurants including the Rainbow Room, The Supper Club, Coco Pazzo Teatro, and Les Halles. The CIA's website goes on to say that he ate his way around the globe in 2000 and released the book *A Cook's Tour*, which later turned into a Food Network series. He authored several other books including his famous *Kitchen Confidential, Nasty Bits, Bone in the Throat, Gone Bamboo,* a graphic novel called *Get Jiro!,* several cookbooks, and essays. He also starred in several TV shows: Travel Channel's *The Layover,* and *CNN's Parts Unknown.* He was awarded culinary accolades including induction into the James Beard Foundation's Who's Who of Food & Beverage, numerous James Beard awards, Emmys, Critics Choice awards, a Clio, a Peabody, and a Webby.

So why was this decorated chef found hanging in his hotel room at the height of his career?

Surely, there are multiple contributing factors, and it's likely that depression, drug use, mental illness and the public pressures of his business were all factors, building up like compound interest. But deeper, and probably most prominent, was a lack of balance in the professional accolades of his career and his personal fulfillment as a human being. Bourdain was chasing momentum, threw himself into the next thing, and was an incredible success. But he ended up paying the ultimate price.

His critical mistake, one many entrepreneurs unfortunately make, is that he tied his happiness to achievement, outcomes, goals—*not* his process. This will either make or break an entrepreneurial venture: If we focus on happiness only "if/when X happens," or think *I'll finally relax when we close this big new client,* you're focusing on the wrong elements.

I meet an endless number of founders. Multiple per day. Dozens per week. The majority of them are drained, overworked, collecting similar industry-level accolades, running multiple companies, and juggling being a parent, a spouse, or a friend.

Though not always at the same level, they' re collectively adding that negative compound interest to their lives. And it shows.

The list of entrepreneurs who have died by confirmed or suspected suicide continues to lengthen. Unfiltered founder Jake Millar. Anti-virus software pioneer John McAfee. Handbag designer Kate Spade, to name a few. Then there are those such as Zappos founder Tony Hsieh, whose mental health is likely also a factor.

Many entrepreneurs and key leaders have declining physical or mental health and deteriorating personal and professional relationships. This has unfortunately become the standard of entrepreneurship and the life of a founder.

James Clear, author of *New York Times*-bestseller *Atomic Habits*, displays this compounding interest factor in his chapter about implementing small changes in the day-to-day:

> *When you fall in love with the **process** rather than the **product**, you don't have to wait to give yourself permission to be happy.*[6]

This small, seemingly insignificant shift can have a compounding effect in the positive or the negative.

---

[6] Bold added.

Own It. Period

When I was in college, I did what many college kids do. I drank a little too much and partied a little too hard. I didn't care enough about what I put in my body and didn't consistently exercise. I stayed relatively "thin" because I barely had enough money to purchase food. Too many times, I'd come home from the bar with an unknown amount of money left in my purse, and that was the amount I had for food that week. I would stare at the remaining $7 (if I were lucky) and feel shame that I'd prioritized going out and partying instead of thinking ahead enough to feed myself that week. That small, seemingly insignificant decision had a compound effect. Going out and having a good time once in a while was not a problem, but it became a habit. Every week. Multiple times per week.

Those behaviors and decisions led to other poor outcomes.

Since I didn't have enough money to buy food, I often didn't buy anything nourishing, and I often stole food from the local grocery store. I would simply toss it in my large tote and walk out the front door. It felt *horrible.* The amount of times I embarrassingly paid for a meal at Checkers drive-in with the spare change I had in my car is astounding.

Soon, I became a person I didn't like. One who couldn't afford to give to others because I could barely give to myself. I was living in a state of myosis, it was all about the here and now—no forward thinking, no reflection, no proactivity. I woke up some days depressed, thinking about all the things I *should* have been learning in college, watching others progress, finding academic and career success.

I had a small blue Honda Civic that my parents had graciously given to me when I turned 17. I took it to college and, with no money, never bothered to keep up with maintenance.

Time after time when I saw the oil change reminder on my windshield, I ignored it, thinking that there was no way I could afford $20 for an oil change. I was embarrassed to admit to my parents that I needed help paying (probably because I'd have to admit that I'd already spent my money at the bar).

One afternoon, I was driving with my now-husband and our friend Grayson, and my car started smoking while I was going over 70 mph down the highway. I caught Grayson's eyes in the rear-view mirror, noting the sheer panic in his face. I quickly pulled off to the side of the highway as the smoke became thick and black.

We scrambled out of the car and stood to the side, watching as smoke poured out of the engine on the side of a bustling New Jersey highway. I could barely breathe through the smoke, and I thought: *Why is this happening **to** me?*

I felt like a victim. I would go to the store, feel bad for myself for not being able to afford food, feel bad that I had to say no to things that I wanted to do because of lack of money, time, or resources. I blamed school for my lack of income, lack of quality time with friends and family, and so much more. *And now*, I thought, *I won't have a working car.*

I blamed everyone. . . but me.

I felt that the outcomes of my life were outside of my control, that success or money or anything I wanted in life had to be given to me by someone or something else. My small inputs seemed insignificant—saying no to going out and staying in to study seemed like a small drop that couldn't possibly affect the big bucket of my life.

Now that I look back, I know I was afraid to take ownership over my failures. It was easy to blame school, blame my financial situation, blame the friend who called me to come to a party. It was *far* harder to look in the mirror and come to terms with the fact that the only common factor was *me*. In my mind, I was a victim to everything happening around me, and I felt stuck.

But then one day, my mom sent me a gift. (I'm one of 5 children, and my mom's always sending us little gifts at the exact right moment, usually with a special word like "joy" painted or stitched onto the gift.)

This day, when I unwrapped the gift, it sure had words, and I'll never forget them:

"Life isn't about finding yourself; it's about creating yourself."

I sat stunned. Just looking at this little wooden thing that may have sat in the sale section of a Home Goods 6 months ago.

These 9 words changed my entire perspective around the power I had in my life. I began to see myself as the author of my story, the person at the helm of my life. I could no longer wait for life, for opportunity, to find me. I had to go create the story I wanted to be part of.

I worked with a client back in early 2019 who came to us because he had no clear processes, no job descriptions for his team, and no path to escaping the stressful cycle he was trapped in.

In our very first discovery call, he said something I'll never forget.

"Alyson, I have no idea what data to look at, and I'm afraid to find it."

Catch that? He was *afraid*. He knew things weren't pretty. Instead of owning the mess and committing to change, he'd been sitting there in a downward spiral, doing nothing, for years.

This client had been hoping to prime his business so he could pass on his legacy to his son. Instead, he ended up selling.

The team (many were members of his family) was so burnt out from so many false starts, none of them had the drive or the desire to take over. We helped him prepare for acquisition, but he felt like he had failed at something it took him 20 years to build.

If you don't own your shit and move in a direction that will lead you to the life and the impact you desire, the damage can sometimes become unbearable. There are a couple of ways to own your own stuff: Sometimes we need to reassess what we think is important or critical in our life and our business. And, sometimes, we just need someone to help us get things moving in the right direction. So, let me help you.

> Truth: You can re-invent, iterate, broaden your horizons, and expand to whatever you desire as long as you have the courage to do one thing: Own it. Own the good and the bad. Own the trouble and the success.

Standard Operating Procedures Are the Answer

So, if you feel anything like Anthony Bourdain—stressed to the max, with "small" issues beginning to compound—step one is to take ownership, realize it's up to you to do something. Next, you need to make a plan to change. You could probably figure this out on your own, but why not learn from the mistakes and successes of others?

Clear, repeatable, and scalable operating structures are the ticket, the escape from a cycle of stress that can never change.

The majority of the owners who collaborate with us have an incredible skill set. They. . .

- Are out-of-this-world service providers
- Can code like no one's business
- Have innovative product development acumen.

So, sometime before coming to me, armed with their skill, they've taken the entrepreneurial leap, to start providing their solution in a crowded and overwhelming marketplace. Through hustle and grit, they gained some traction, and voila, they became a business owner.

And then, one day, they find themselves responding to fires, managing team members, and wholly reactive to a business that they feel imprisoned by. Quickly, the skill that they were originally (and in some cases still are) good at, becomes secondary to a hungry beast that eats up all their time and resources. There's no obvious solution to them—it's hard to read the label from inside the bottle.

Imagine training a horse, a wild animal, that's incredibly capable and stubborn. Left to its own devices, it'll run off on its own, requiring hundreds of hours to wrangle it in. A business is no different. It can take on a mind of its own (as a sum of its parts) and start to run off the rails if we don't give it the operating guidelines. We need to get out of the day-to-day to properly assess and implement solutions.

Instead of being a slave to the business you've created—which now seems to have complete control over you—give it a routine and structure. Tell it how you'd like it to behave, and what you expect of it. I know it may sound simple, but guess what? It actually can be (but it does take time and commitment).

Just like everything worth doing, training this wild beast into a thoroughbred that performs often takes some time and difficult readjustments before things become easier.

The good news is, you can start to make operational changes immediately that help you tame the beast. Because operations used to only be accessible to the corporations who had enough budget to be able to afford all this fancy Six Sigma training and leadership retreats, many founders and small-business owners think that operations = red tape. Months of approval for anything to actually get done, a seemingly endless chain of command. And it stops many of us small-business owners right in our tracks because we are, in function, anti-corporate. But using some of their secrets isn't all bad. It's what helps them grow and dominate their market and change CEOs every few years. The business is tamed, and it's not dependent on any one person.

Developing clear operational structure in your business is the absolute key to creating the balance that you desire. The Sabbatical Method will help make clear what you need to develop as part of your journey, give you a break in the meantime, and help you create operational practices that afford you more and more rest. It's a constant filter for upleveling or sustaining what you've created.

With the Sabbatical Method implemented into your business, you can access something that every top-performing CEOs will tell you is the main factor that contributes to their company's success—time to work *on* their business, generating new ideas for its growth. On top of that, adding routine sabbatical time into your work-life will give you longevity and peace. There will be fewer urgent fires to deal with, for one. Plus, no more going into quarters blind or looking back at the yearly goals and wondering why they weren't hit. No more leaving on vacation and getting bombarded with hundreds of emails. No more dependence on any one employee.

Invitation to the Sabbatical Method

Over the next 90-days, I'd like you to work with me to create a plan for your sabbatical. This sabbatical will probably *not* mean you're going to entirely remove yourself from your business immediately.[7] Rather, the goal is to change your current role in the business, so it begins to serve you and become the increasingly independent business you want it to be.

In each chapter ahead, we're going to work on the core habits and activities you need to focus on to say goodbye to your old role in your company and hello to your new one. This is going to be hard. You will likely be tempted to jump back into old ways, either out of urgency or habit. But you must commit to being better, to use every instance where you get pulled in to "put out a fire" as an opportunity, not a setback.

Let me say that again: anything bad that happens in your business is an opportunity, an opportunity to learn more about how to handle stress, empower team members, and create systems that will prevent these situations from recurring.

Along the way, I'm going to encourage you to use new tools and systems and exercise tough love with your team to equip them to handle problems while you ascend to another level in your business.

Too often, I meet owners on the brink of burnout and teams who are so disconnected they can barely bring projects over the finish line. I'm tired of it. Like many of the things worth doing in life: the solutions are simple and challenging. If we want to

---

[7] Even though I frequently help owners plan for these types of sabbaticals.

stay in business, if we want to build longevity, we need to do hard things. We need to do the unsexy work that is going to keep our businesses surviving and thriving without all our blood, sweat, and tears for eternity. So, here's my commitment to you:

I'll give you everything necessary to succeed in 90 days—the tactics, the tools, the motivation, the knowledge, so that you can create the habits you need to succeed in your new Sabbatical Method.

Now, let's get to work.

Yours operationally.

Summary:

- When business owners blindly hustle, working toward the next goal, eventually, their entire business will become unsustainable.
- Fall in love with the process, not the outcomes.
- It's up to business owners to own our individual habits and create systems to support our lives and our businesses.

The Sabbatical Method: Weaving rest into your life on a regular cadence by creating operational systems and processes that create an increasingly independent business.

Critical Action:

Create a crystal-clear, giant intention for yourself. Write it down somewhere you can see it daily. Remind yourself that you alone are the person responsible for changing your situation.

Example: I am committed to living a happier, healthier life for my family and also to the longevity of my business.

CHAPTER 2

THE OPERATIONS, SIMPLIFIED™ HIERARCHY

The 5 Levels of Operational Efficiency

SELF-ACTUALIZATION	PROFIT + PROSPER
ESTEEM	GROWTH + SCALE
LOVE + BELONGINGNESS	QUALITY + COST
SAFETY	EFFICIENCY + IMPROVEMENT
PHYSIOLOGICAL NEEDS	PROCESS CREATION + PLANNING

Mission: Simplify your operations, making standardization easy to implement. Here, I'll show you the 5 core operational levels of a healthy small business and why they matter for creating consistent opportunities for rest.

In 1943, Abraham Maslow created a foundational framework for understanding human desires and resulting behavior. Today, many of us know this framework as "Maslow's Hierarchy of Needs."

Maslow's theory has had a profound impact on the field of psychology, and it's been expanded and applied to a wide range of fields, including education, management, and marketing.

Originally, this theory supposedly came from Maslow's observation of a family of squirrels in his backyard. He noticed that they had a set of needs that were required to be met before they could move onto the next phase in their development. To him, and many thereafter, the hierarchy of needs is a filter or a rubric we can use to diagnose specific behaviors based on what is lacking in individual development.

There have certainly been improvements, additions, challengers, and opposers over the years, but his simple framework has stood the test of time.

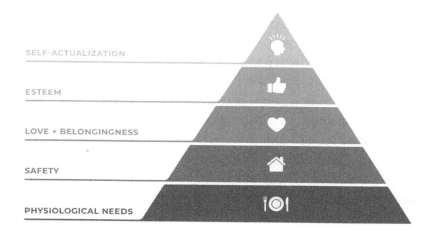

Maslow developed his pyramid of human needs in the early 1940s but became obsessed with self-actualization over the course of his career. He studied various patients and their behaviors in an attempt to understand how human beings reach happiness and contentment. A key to his discoveries was, of course, motivation by a higher purpose. A calling, so to speak.

Maslow also found that the motivation for self-actualization begins early on, not just once everything below has been satisfied, but throughout the human condition beginning as early as stage 2, safety. Clearly, then, one's sense of purpose is a driving force throughout their life, regardless of the "level" they're on.

Maslow also posited in his later work that each stage of the hierarchy is not dependent on the previous being complete entirely. Meaning, we may not have a permanent place to live (typically associated with safety), but we may still be searching for belonging (typically associated with the top level, self-actualization).

I'd studied Maslow's hierarchy in high school, but I had no idea the impact it would have on my business and how I served my clients until I hired Madison.

In late 2018, I'd been working on my own at the Operations Agency for over a year. Mostly providing fractional work to founders in the growth phases of their businesses, I was involved with some really cool projects. I did numerous events and launched new impactful memberships, coaching programs, books, workshops. . . . You name it, I did it. I was the sweaty generalist of the ops industry, and lots of people wanted to hire me for my time, which was great, but this presented a problem for me: I was working all the time. I only had the capacity for a handful of clients if I wanted to keep my quality high, which was mission critical for me.

In 2018 I was faced with a decision: to hire someone else, or to cap my client load at just 4 clients and keep raising my prices. I still had doubts about whether I had the chops to be an entrepreneur. (Let's face it, I still have those doubts.) But back then, given the general nature of my work and being a fractional COO, chief of staff, and even an administrative assistant, it was really hard to see myself leading a team of my own and building a company.

Pushing through self-doubt and imposter syndrome, I gingerly made my first hire. Up there with my favorite people I've ever worked with, Madison joined my business as my assistant.

She was tenacious, humble, and hungry and worked in Apple's health clinic at the time. She took a few hours here and there on evenings and weekends and really encouraged me to think through my own process for assessing operational needs for myself and for my clients.

Working with Madison was challenging. In all the good ways. It was challenging to make ends meet, to pay someone, to give them enough to do, to encourage them to grow, and to meet new challenges. In hindsight, I was extremely lucky to have found her when I did, because hiring the wrong person at that time in my growth could have been the difference between expanding Operations Agency and remaining a solopreneur.

I remember one of the first meetings I had with Madison. We went over a client I was working with, the scope of their project, their team members, and what I may need her support with. She asked some great questions about my entire approach.

I knew that operations would help businesses stand the test of time, and I wanted to return founders back to their families without destroying their companies. But, until that point, I had been head-down, working with clients one-by-one, and hadn't ever had to communicate how I helped each client work through their operations. Now, Madison was right there, asking difficult but important questions so she could dive in and take on some of my work and move it to her plate. I had to have specific, standardized answers. Ironically, even for me—a specialist in operations—*my* processes for each client were difficult to spell out for Madison!

This is a pivotal moment in every business. Once we invite someone outside into our world, add a new leader to the team, or create a new department, our business takes on a new life and we *must* think about how we set this new person or entity up for success. We must show them the specific *how.*

Hierarchy of Business Needs

So, based on Madison's questions, I began to write down the general operational needs of businesses. The first version of the Operations, Simplified™ framework was born. Today, I've laid it out more elegantly, with some refinement. Here's how it looks:

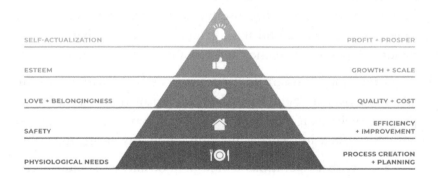

Each piece of the Operations, Simplified™ Hierarchy represents an operational level or set of levels that a business needs to achieve self-actualization. By utilizing this approach, the business can become independent of any one person, and you can systematically achieve goals in the company, improve customer experience, launch new products, you name it. I've used these 5 levels to help companies assess their operational health whether they are a 2-person shop or a 500-employee organization. The principles are always the same.

At each level of a business, I've paired it with one of Maslow's levels. As you probably know, these aren't really levels like you're playing a game—you don't "complete" one and then move onto the next. I've worked with businesses that are doing alright with some higher levels, but they're struggling with a more foundational one. But the reason they're in the order they're in, is each one below typically has an outsized effect on all layers above it.

For instance, if you're struggling with every level, then once you correct the most foundational one (Level 1: Process Creation & Planning), then, likely, you'll have automatically corrected problems in the other areas.

Later, we'll help you identify gaps in your company to determine where your improvement efforts will be most effective. For now, let's just break each one down.

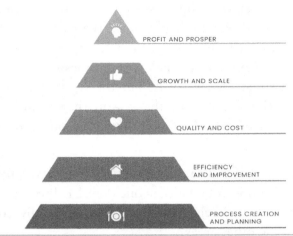

PROFIT AND PROSPER

GROWTH AND SCALE

QUALITY AND COST

EFFICIENCY AND IMPROVEMENT

PROCESS CREATION AND PLANNING

OPERATIONAL OBJECTIVE 5: PULL BACK THE CURTAIN
ACTIONS:
1) FIND FULFILLMENT IN THE IMPACT YOU ARE MAKING.
2) HAVE A BUSINESS THAT'S INDEPENDENT OF ANY ONE PERSON'S INPUT, INCLUDING YOUR OWN.

OPERATIONAL OBJECTIVE 4: DO MORE WITH MORE
ACTIONS:
1) USE A PROVEN STRATEGY AND PROCESS FOR GROWTH.
2) DEVELOP A CLEAR WAY TO ASSESS CAPACITY RELATING TO QUALITY AND COST.

OPERATIONAL OBJECTIVE 3: STAY IN SCOPE
ACTIONS:
1) ENSURE CONSISTENT QUALITY THROUGHOUT THE BUSINESS.
2) REGULATE QUALITY AT A CONSISTENT COST.

OPERATIONAL OBJECTIVE 2: MOVE FASTER AND MORE ACCURATELY
ACTIONS:
1) CREATE CONSISTENCY.
2) HABITUAL IMPROVEMENT.

OPERATIONAL OBJECTIVE 1: FULFILL BASIC BUSINESS NEEDS
ACTIONS:
1) CREATE A WAY TO CONSISTENTLY CREATE PROCESSES.
2) CREATE A CONSISTENT WAY TO PLAN, TRACK, AND ACHIEVE GROWTH INITIATIVES.

Level 1: Process Creation + Planning

Operational Objective 1: Fulfill basic business needs

Actions: 1) Create a way to consistently create processes. 2) Generate a consistent way to plan, track, and achieve growth initiatives.

This level is a delicate balance that all organizations need to get right before they dream of having any repeatable, scalable outcomes. Process creation refers to the way businesses get results and then turn those results into repeatable processes. Consider how our cars are maintained: we get an oil change every 10,000 miles or so, we change the air filters a little less often and, every once in a while, we get the brakes assessed and changed. How and when those actions are performed are critical to the functionality of your vehicle, just like creating and maintaining processes in your business. Everything you are doing to keep the business running should be documented and turned into a repeat process. And, more, there needs to be a process for creating processes. There needs to be a clear-cut (and quick) way to get every action that is completed more than 2 or 3 times down onto paper.

Planning is the second important ingredient of this objective. Because if we're not growing, we're dying. Small businesses should be breaking things. That's their job. What we want to have woven into the foundation for how we operate is a way to consistently plan growth initiatives without them taking our business over completely or just dying by the wayside. If we can master this balance at the different growth points of our business, we'll be on our way to outlasting our competition.

**

There's a man who lives in my neighborhood whose consistency I admire. We cross paths every morning between 6:30 and 7:30 am when I'm headed out to our home gym.

He has a beautiful blue-nose pit bull that he walks... every single day, twice. I see him out in the rain, in the snow, or with a pending storm on the horizon. Each morning I catch him, smile, wave, and say good morning. He returns each time with a booming return salutation and a comment about how wonderful the day is—even if it's absolutely treacherous outside.

Consider this in terms of your business—his dedication and rigor are his SOPs or "Standard Operating Procedures." For you, it's time to create some non-negotiables for your business's daily habits.

At level 1, Maslow discusses the basic human need for food, water, shelter. That's what SOPs are for your business: the basic inputs that keep the lights on and things running healthily.

I was interviewing a mompreneur (Renée) on my podcast recently who had just attended Tony Robbins' event *Become Unshakable*. The 5 full days of the event are brutal. Dawn until dusk. You barely sleep, and you're in sessions most of the time. Standing, listening, absorbing. Doing challenging activities.

I imagine Tony Robbins events to be like mini boot camps for the soul. I asked Renée—who's a mom of 2 boys, owns a PR business, and is married to the man who's the leading SaaS[8] founder coach in the world—what she leaned on to thrive during those long days. Her reply was super interesting:

"I focused on the fuel I put in my body. I drank an ample amount of water and ate food I knew would give me the energy to keep going."

Simple. Elegant. Just like the small answers that can help fuel your business.

We tend to overcomplicate things when we take a look under the hood. We're biased because we think, since we're smart, if we haven't figured out operations already, it all must be complicated. It isn't. It's all about breaking bad habits, optimizing

---

[8] Software as a Service

good ones, and starting needed ones. To generate more leads, you may need to be featured in more media; to close more sales you may need to do more cold calling. Plenty of tried-and-true tactics are simple and uncomplicated.

We'll dive into this a little deeper in Chapter 4, but take my word for it: your basic business needs are likely as simple as Renee's were for getting through her long days with Tony Robbins.

Level 2: Efficiency + Improvement

Operational Objective 2: Move faster and more accurately

Actions: 1) Create consistency. 2) Have habitual improvement.

Once we determine what the basic functions of our business are, the next logical problem that gets created is moving faster or more accurately. I'll call these repeatable, scalable outcomes. We can be the best process documenters in the entire world, but those mean little if we can't create repeatable outcomes. If we can't create a repeatable process for these outcomes, it becomes impossible to guarantee performance because simply put, there are too many variables.

Writing down your process is the first step, but how that process transfers to another and another is how it becomes repeatable.

If you're looking to grow a company to the point of exit, this is a huge element for you to pay attention to, because, in my experience, it's the most important factor to the sale of a business, after cash flow. Buyers want to see that there is value in your process, that it exists outside of any one person, and that if it's repeated at scale, it's going to make them more money.

The best thing we can do for our business is to get those processes down on paper, then tie metrics that can measure those outcomes.

By the way, I'm not saying to create a repeat process and never change it. That's absurd. Growing businesses are supposed to break things. It's iterative. It's in the DNA. But what we can do is put the process on one side of an equation, and a metric on the other to see if how we change the process improves or crushes the outcome we're trying to achieve.

For example, let's say you're a software company owner and you want to respond to and solve customer service inquiries in under 24 business hours. That's a great goal and likely needs a process (or several) to support a team to achieve that result.

You could write out a checklist or make some requirements for working hours and see how the metric is affected. You may write out email templates for the team or set up some automation in the first interaction with the customer and see how the metric is affected.

But if you keep updating your processes without checking to see if they improve overall performance, it's like having a goal to lose weight, then changing your diet and never hopping on the scale.

That's why metrics are important. They help you eventually determine: "If X is repeated, will I achieve the results I want, at scale?"

I had a client once who ran a branding agency. He did a ton of custom design work, wireframing, built websites, the whole 9 yards. Operationally, he functioned much more like a full-service agency because he was also giving his clients sales and marketing coaching behind the scenes. This guy did it all.

Right before we sat down together to work on his processes, he decided to launch some productized versions of his services at a lower price to help capture part of his market that couldn't afford to work with him previously.

I'm a genius, he probably thought.

When these "productized" services sold like gangbusters, he and his team didn't know what to do. They only had practice delivering on their usual high-ticket, high-touch experiences. They had no idea how to generate similar results with double the client load (most of whom were now paying a fraction of the price).

When he came to me, he told me he *might* break even on these new engagements. My encouragement to him was to start small with a few clients, get the process down, and then repeat it at scale. Of course, I wanted him to grow—and I love the enthusiastic, no-holds-barred approach, as those moves can bring a fast cash injection into a business.

But an influx of cash means absolutely nothing if you're going to spend more to keep it. You can chalk it up to a learning experience, but it'll be a costly one.

We've all been in positions where we have to say no to something that we don't have the capacity for. We've also likely all been in a position where we said yes to something we probably shouldn't have, maybe because our business simply wasn't ready to execute on it.

Just as Maslow's corresponding level here is "safety," we also need to create safety in our business, by having measurable metrics that allow us to make accurate decisions about which new opportunities to say yes to. . . without everything falling apart behind the scenes.

You get that safety by 1) creating consistency around projects and 2) standardizing project timelines and outcomes.

Level 3: Quality + Cost

Operational Objective 3: Stay in scope

Actions: 1) Ensure consistent quality throughout the business. 2) Regulate quality at a consistent cost.

Staying within the crosshairs of cost and quality is critical to understanding how to structure your operations. One of the many reasons I've situated this objective parallel to Maslow's "love and belonging" is because if we get this right, we'll create lifelong raving fans of our business.

Cost and quality are areas where I see companies who do have operational structure defined still get things wrong—because they aren't clear on the core pieces of their product or service, they add new things that they think their market wants in order to create more revenue. This is a no-no. It's really likely that improving something you're already doing will yield the best outcome at the lowest cost. In other words, for the most ROI, most business leaders should refine their current offerings instead of creating new ones.

One of the biggest takeaways to remember here is that you don't need to reinvent the wheel. Often just creating a communication structure with your customers can increase the perceived level of quality or customization without increasing expenses. And customers are just one of the 3 groups of "our people," which I typically break down into these important categories:

A: Customers

We want to create an experience for our customers that keeps them around. We want them to rave about how amazing our business solution is. This isn't easy—it takes repetition, iteration, and a little magic from you, as you pull back the curtain and give them a taste of who you and your team really are.

If you've ever stayed in a Ritz Carlton hotel, you know the type of vibe I'm talking about—you're surprised, delighted, and fully supported at every turn. The opportunity to engage with the Ritz Carlton brand during your stay is seemingly endless, which makes sense, as their mission statement is, "Luxury without limits."

And the cool thing about being anywhere in the Ritz Carlton atmosphere—whether you're staying in one of their rooms, dining at one of their restaurants, refining your backhand at one of their tennis lessons, or playing at the pool with an à la carte day pass—is that you get a *taste* of the experience at whichever level you're at.

Through-and-through, Ritz Carlton is a luxury experience, but they manage expectations at every level: There's no expectation that someone purchasing a tennis lesson or coming to the pool for the day is going to be given a surprise hotel room. The customer expects to receive a fantastic tennis lesson from a world-renowned brand, and Ritz Carlton delivers. And, that fantastic experience leaves the customer wanting *more* of the same-quality experience.

Once, an agency told me that his baseline web service wasn't profitable. When I asked why, he said, "They expect that we're going to roll out the red carpet for them like we do with our white-glove clients."

I asked a quick follow up:

"Do they *expect* that, or do *you default* to that behavior?"

He paused and pondered. A lightbulb had gone off.

Instead of giving his baseline web service clients a taste of the red carpet, a media pass of sorts the same way Ritz Carlton does, he was defaulting to giving them the experience of his high-paying clients, because that's all he knew how to do.

Ritz Carlton not only provides incredible guest service at every level, but they also manage expectations at these levels, and therefore, costs. Likewise, we need to think through the unique experience of our clients at every level.

Creating a home for customers, making them feel like they belong, is the most surefire way to create raving fans in the marketplace and pad the bottom line with repeat customers who can go out in the world and generate new business for us.

B: Team

The second important group in your "people" category is your team.

You need to hear this:

> People will always be your most expensive line item in your business.

And if you're reading this without having built a team yet: The team is you. You're the expense.

It is mission critical to make sure they (or you) understand what they're doing and how to do it.

You don't want to end up in a position where you're paying for someone's time and they don't know what's expected of them or how to complete the tasks you've delegated (or are trying to delegate) to them.

You can't afford to not support your team, for at least 2 reasons:

1. **You're paying more for their time if they're not efficient and passionate about what they do.**

   If your team has the resources, they need to do their job well (SOPs, clear metrics, clear responsibilities, a feedback loop with their leadership and direct reports, etc.), they'll be more valuable to your business. If they feel like their job is a vehicle for their personal growth and aspirations, you've hit the jackpot.

   Why not do both?

   Talk to your team. Ask if they need support, clarity, or certainty to do their job, even just a little better. I talk with my team about this at least once per quarter.

   Then, ask them what they want in their personal lives and how you could structure their work around those aspects. Remember: It's not just all about the money. I've had plenty of employees ask me to do a "not so full time" schedule to be with their families more. Then, they show up ready to get shit done with the time they've dedicated to me.

2. **You're at risk of losing good people if you don't support them.**

   If you have good people, keep them. Support them. When good employees leave, they take valuable knowledge and experience (and sometimes relationships) with them.

Vacancies created by good workers are especially painful when the "how" piece is up in their head and not down on paper.

We're all aware of the cost of re-staffing. No bueno.

Something simple you can do this week with your team is schedule one-on-one meetings. Ask each team member what their personal aspirations are and how the company can support those. Great news is, you can co-create a plan to get there.

***

One caveat to this point: Don't live in fear, letting this point keep you from hiring people altogether. People are the most valuable part of your business. . . just treat them like it.

C: Community

The third important group in your "people" category is your community—those who will make things a little simpler for you and support your personal and professional growth, such as coaches, consultants, partners, and colleagues. These people pour into your business and allow you to take shortcut strategies because they've walked where you've walked, and they can tell you which trail to get on, which to avoid, and where the potholes are.

Anytime I've ever tried to "go it alone" without the support of this group, I've failed. Miserably. I don't do that anymore. I find the "who," as business thought leader Dan Sullivan says.

Teams have coaches to lead them to victories.

Mafia Dons have consiglieres.

Successful marketing includes an element of partnering.

If you aren't teamed up with a group of people you're working with, drawing support from, and offering your own talents to, something's off.

You can't afford not to partake in a community. Without the valuable experience of others, you'll still learn the lessons, but they'll end up costing you far more money. There's also a ton of research around the psychology of investing in yourself and how it encourages people to step into new levels of leadership and commitment.

My coach, Emily, is one of the best investments I've ever made. Why? It's not because she has million-dollar business tactics or because she refers me to a ton of clients. Rather, It's because I invest in myself every month. Deep in my subconscious, there's now a voice that echoes every time one of those payments goes through from my account to her: *I'm worth it. I'm a solid investment.*

So, a note to those who don't believe they deserve any of this: Consider this your wakeup call. You do.

Bottom line: Invest in your clients, invest in your team, and invest in yourself. You'll build a world-class culture that people can't wait to join.

Level 4: Growth + Scale

Operational Objective 4: Do more with more

Actions: 1) Use a proven strategy and process for growth. 2) Develop a clear way to assess capacity relating to quality and cost.

Let's say this one together: "*Growth* and *scale* do not mean the same thing!"

Often, at level 4, my clients and I discuss the idea of "feast or famine." When I'm assessing a business and observe that they have a pendulum that oscillates between high sales one month and low sales the next, I know they're able to *grow* but not *scale*.

Growth simply means "influx." If you're reading this, you're probably a founder, which means you're likely great at selling. Closing new business probably comes second nature to you. The problem is what happens afterward. Can you keep consistent results when you continue to pile on more and more? Often, the answer is no.

When I focus on this level with my clients, most critically, we're looking at capacity planning:

- How much work, or how many projects or customers, can the business truly handle?
- What are the indicators to consider before it's too late and the business needs to retract?

No business wants to be investing heavily in their company's growth, purchasing resources, hiring new team members, and paying for new equipment, to then suddenly find themselves unable to deliver against the weight of new sales or sales projections. That'll crush your business, putting everyone out of a job.

You can make the prettiest playbooks and organize tons of good information about what's happening with your business, but once the flood gates open and you begin growing the reach to new markets and closing more business... things get tested.

I once worked with an organization that was stuck at $1.5 million in revenue. For 3 years.

They tried everything, and every time the founders (the leaders in closing new business) would sell more services, they were losing more money than they were bringing in. Why?

When we looked under the hood, they had knowledgeable, hard-working employees, but most were working in department- or individual- level silos. No one communicated to one another, they had different ways of running their individual projects, and there was no unified way to review outputs of departments.

Overall, the employees had no idea what was going on, and the founders were frustrated. Truthfully, they just wanted to grow the company as quickly as possible so they could sell it for the highest dollar amount. So, they would jump in and tackle tasks for team members, which would raise the fulfillment cost significantly, negating their hard work. Trying to grow revenue without focusing on streamlining fulfillment is frustrating, to say the least; it's like a snake eating its own tail. As I said:

Growth is influx. Scale is doing more with more. Or, ideally, more with less.

The more technical definition of scale, as told by Tony Robbins, is "to increase revenue at a faster rate than costs."

A scorecard is critical at this stage: if we haven't rolled our metrics into one location that we review with our team(s) weekly, we're going to wake up one morning and everything will be on fire.

Scorecards

A scorecard is a window into how your team is operating. You may add your quarterly or annual goals to a document or into a project management tool, but your scorecard is what tracks the metrics related to those outcomes.

For instance, let's say that a goal for one quarter is to decrease the amount of time it takes on onboarding new customers from 14 to 4 days. You could leverage a scorecard to create this outcome in 3 phases:

1. Measure how long it currently takes your team to onboard a customer (in a project management tool, customer relationship management system, etc.).
2. Ensure there is one person dedicated to this metric, who eats, sleeps, and breathes onboarding to make things more efficient and beneficial to the customer.
3. Make this metric (time to onboard) visible for the team for review at every single weekly huddle.

You can't improve what you don't measure. So, measure it *weekly*. Why weekly? Simply put, I want 52 chances a year to pivot.

If we review our critical metrics weekly, we train our team to be results-focused and we reinforce that these metrics matter and that we want to use critical thinking skills to solve problems together.

Systems for Decisions

But perhaps the most important operational muscle a business can build at level 4, is the art of confident, rapid decision-making.

Think of air traffic control: They have seemingly infinite decisions to make—when to land, which runway to use, what altitude and speed planes should fly at, etc. I'm exhausted just thinking and considering all the elements that are at play for air traffic control operators.

The reason air traffic controllers don't quit after an hour of being up in their towers is because they have systems for how they make those decisions. They monitor metrics and look at the overall status of key important elements to help them along. The other key to their stamina is that the options aren't infinite. Many decisions require either a yes or a no, or one of similarity limited choices:

- Is the weather safe preflight?
- Can we take off?
- At what altitude are we cruising?
- Can we descend?
- Can we land? Where?

These seem like complex questions, but in practice, there are checklists, processes, and/or metrics that inform each of these decisions at scale. Every day, the US operates over 25,000 flights—that's a colossal amount of decisions. Frankly, it's too many for air traffic controllers to make without systems. For them, these systems are mission critical.

And that's the key to scaling: having systems that tell you accurately how things are going, offering you accurate data and allowing you to make the right decisions for your business.

Level 5: Profit + Prosper

Operational Objective 5: Pull back the curtain

Actions: 1) Find fulfillment in the impact you're making. 2) Run a business that's independent of any one person's input, including your own.

When I was a little girl, I was convinced that I wanted to be a travel blogger and critic.

When we would vacation as a family, I would always think about how interesting it would be to get a "free" vacation by paying attention to what was happening around me, write down my opinions, then go on to the next place.

The problem with my travel blogger plan was that it didn't include making life better for anyone else but myself. It was selfish. I wanted a free vacation, and I wanted to sit and write (which I love doing) from a poolside in Punta Cana because I thought it'd be fun. But there was no purpose. No deep-seeded reason why this would benefit another individual or group of people. What makes businesses interesting and even more wildly successful after scaling is the level of an impact and the market-penetration of your solution: the more people who have it, the greater your impact. In other words, your business should speak to your self-actualization.

Self-actualization in Maslow's terms is the desire to become the most that one can be. *The most.*

In my perspective, a founder's self-actualization boils down to 2 critical questions:

1. *How can I spend most of my days doing exactly what I want?*
2. *How can I make the most impact with the solution I provide?*

When we're in self-actualization mode, or "prospering" as I call it, we live in that sweet spot of working hard on the things that matter and actually enjoying the process. In his book, *The Big Leap*, psychologist Gay Hendricks calls this the "Zone of Genius." Simply put, if you're truly prospering, you're doing what you love *and* making an impact on others.

At this stage of business, you get to ask yourself: *How far can this thing go? How many people do I want to serve? How deep of an impact am I trying to make?*

Optimizing how you spend your time is critical to the longevity of your business. If you (and the bulk of your leadership team) are operating in your "Zone of Genius" or prospering, you know that there's a much larger chance that the organization will stay in business longer and have the trajectory to accomplish incredible things. So, ask yourself:

After I've grown to the point I've always dreamed, do I want to do this every day?

Sure, there will be seasons of difficulty, but the key is to ensure that you're actually enjoying the work you're doing, and that your solutions solve as many problems for as many customers as possible.

Here, I often tell my clients to create a 3-year picture of their organization and of their role in it.

Tony Robbins (I really appreciate him, if that's not obvious!) does the same routine every day. [9]He wakes up, practices meditation and does yoga, trains with his physical trainer, has a protein shake, eats breakfast, attends important team meetings, spends time with his family, eats dinner, sleeps. [10]

If I didn't mention this was Tony's routine, you may have mistaken it for your own. There's nothing incredibly unique about it: he's a human being. He needs most of those things to survive and thrive. The beauty is that he enjoys his days, as he's worked himself out of the core functions of his operations. Tony did some tremendously hard work to grow an incredibly impactful organization and now, he's simply behind the wheel, steering

---

[9] 1. "What Tony Robbins Does Every Morning," YouTube, November 16, 2017, https://www.youtube.com/watch?v=VXYhfy4b5Bg.

[10] 1. Richard Feloni, "Tony Robbins Explains What Anyone Can Do Every Day, Month, and Year to Be More Successful," Business Insider, June 30, 2017, https://www.businessinsider.com/tony-robbins-day-month-year-exercises-2017-7.

the ship in the direction he knows will be most impactful, making decisions that will truly matter to the growth of his organization.

Tony is proof that you can lead 50 companies and have a $5 billion empire *and* enjoy your life. If we pull back the curtain, we see him doing what he always does. And he's not applying a profound strategy. It's simple. He focuses on internal growth first, external growth second. Apply this to your own life, at your own revenue point.

I want you to become more like Tony. I want to help you create days, weeks, months, and years of your life that you can enjoy. Limitless impact and limitless joy. Too often, entrepreneurs spend their days bogged down in the operations of their businesses because no one gives them the practical tools to structure things, *simply*. My hope is that in just a short, 90-day period, we can change the trajectory of your business, how you spend your time, increase how much time and energy you devote to your family and make an impact in your community. Together, we can change everything. If you're willing to show up and do the hard work to get there, this book will help you take action toward creating the same operational infrastructure as some of the largest, most impactful companies of our time.

It all starts with how you spend your days and the decisions you position in front of yourself.

They Aren't Really Levels

Like Maslow first thought, I originally believed that these phases were strictly building blocks, level 1 leading to level 2, and so on. And, in some ways, they are. But in the last 5 years of refining the framework and running clients through the process, I've come to realize that we can put our business through this assessment at any point in its existence, and businesses can struggle with an "earlier" level, even if they're at a higher one.

Once, a client whom we'll call "Charles" came to me while he was at Level 5: Profit & Prosper. He had marketplace notoriety, he was achieving amazing results for his clients, and he had repeatability, scalability, and many other important aspects of his business figured out. But he was missing one basic thing: delegation.

In order to protect his own image, he'd created a fictitious assistant named "Mary." Mary was really just Charles, responding to all his own emails. He'd made it all the way to the highest level of actualization in his business, but still couldn't take a family vacation without pretending to be Mary. He was living his whole life like the Wizard of Oz, hoping no one would pay attention to the man behind the curtain.

As I've said, while each level at the bottom of the pyramid typically makes the one above it much easier to achieve, you can have gaps in a variety of areas, or even in only one at a lower level. So, I now have all my clients use this pyramid as an assessment tool to gauge where the gaps may be:

- How well do your employees understand company initiatives? Do they have a central location to access the information they need to achieve the outcomes they're responsible for?
- Are the basic needs of the business and the individuals within your business covered on a daily basis?
- Do you have a consistent method of tracking outcomes?
- Are projects consistent?
- Does everyone understand their role?
- How much capacity do you have for new work? At which point will something break?

In the later chapters we're going to explore the steps you need to take for each level of the business. But for now, your chapter-ending Critical Action is simple. I want you to get a firm grasp on the gaps that may exist within your business. Follow the Critical Action at the end of this chapter to take my assessment.

Together, we're going to make a plan to work you out of the job you currently have and professionalize each area of your business at every level. In the next chapter, we'll discuss some simple habits you can implement to start you down the right path. Each chapter will break down, in detail, what to think through and tackle if you find yourself needing support in one (or more) of all the operational levels.

Also, I want to remind you: I made a toolkit just for you. It has all the templates, checklists, tips, tricks, and in-depth videos to help you and your team through this journey. Get it at thesab-baticalmathod.com/toolkit

Yours operationally.

Summary:

- Human beings have fundamental needs to survive and thrive; businesses have similar operational needs.
- There are 5 core operational levels for a small business, which I call, Operations, Simplified™.
- We're going to use these 5 levels to assess where you need to focus your time during your sabbatical.
- Each level has an associated objective, along with 1 or 2 specific actions that are mission critical to your company's overall operational health.

Honing these is a lifelong practice. As long as your business is in business, we can aim to improve each area of your company.

Critical Action:

Take the assessment at thesabbaticalmethod.com/ toolkit. This will help you determine the state of operations at your business, and whether it can function without you. This will help you understand where to focus as you work yourself out of your business.

CHAPTER 3

REMODELS START WITH ONE ROOM

The Sabbatical Method Checklist

Mission: Make a plan for your sabbatical. In this chapter, we're going to understand the types of sabbaticals you can take, the habits that will need to be implemented to take them, and who you must become to access the benefits of this method.

In August 2021, my family made a huge decision. We lived just outside of Nashville, Tennessee at the time, and we had discovered the month prior that I was pregnant with our second son. My older son was only 9 months, and it was a shock. We had tried for a baby for just over 2 years before I became pregnant with our first son, Frank, so we assumed that once we started trying for a second, it would take a while. Nope. This time, it only took one month.

I was grateful and excited when I took the test and saw the results, but another, huge part of me was nervous. We had been talking about moving for the last few months, and it was always important to us to be closer to our families once we had a family of our own. Steve and I sat down to discuss. We knew if we didn't move ASAP, we would probably remain in Tennessee for another few years.

So, just 2 weeks after finding out I was pregnant with John, we listed our house. It was only on the market for 3 days before we accepted an offer. And 6 weeks later, we were homeless, driving across the country with our 13-month-old, our dog, and everything we could fit into our Toyota 4Runner.

It was scary. We didn't know what to expect. The market was crazy at the time. Even though we'd just sold our home and received an incredible price for it, we knew we'd be in the buyer seat shortly. And that wasn't a fun seat to be in.

After getting settled at my parent's, we made a list of homes to view and found ourselves a realtor.

It took us 3 and a half months to find, choose, contract, and close on our new home. Prior to closing, we'd made several offers on other homes that were passed over for higher, less contingent offers from other buyers. Some even waiving basic inspection which absolutely baffled us.

We settled in our new home in December 2021. I remember the day we did the walkthrough and signed the papers in a small-town real estate office in Pennsylvania. It was slightly raining and ice cold, but we got in just a few days before the holidays.

After all the obligatory signatures, we shook hands, wished happy holidays, and drove up to our new home.

It was an absolute dump.

Our home was built in the 1980s, and the carpet matched the original build in a lovely shade of putting green. The family who'd previously lived there had 6 (!) children, so they needed all the space they could get firsthand. Our now-laundry room had just been someone's bedroom when we moved in.

To say this was the biggest project we'd ever taken on was an understatement. And remember, we had a new baby on the way. I was due on March 15. So, we had just under 3 months and my husband's set of hands to finish all the things that needed updating before John was born.

Those 3 months are blurry. We ate copious amounts of take-out, because we didn't have a kitchen, and we lived in a construction site. I was waddling all over the place trying to entertain Frank and coordinate material deliveries for our house project, all while keeping my company, Operations Agency, running.

We'd wake up and there'd be a ton of snow on the ground, so deliveries would be delayed. And since we had no kitchen to make food, we'd go to a nearby diner for a cup of coffee and some eggs, sitting just long enough to enjoy the cozy warmth.

The important element that kept both my husband and me sane was this: we had a plan. We put it together prior to our closing, and we knew that if we put in the work, got the material we needed, and added in some buffer time, we'd be OK. Our plan laid out when we needed what material, and the order which we needed to build or repair things. This kept the seeming chaos in order.

In this chapter, we're going to help you take the first step into your Sabbatical Method lifestyle. To do that, we're going to need a plan to get started.

This plan is your jumpstart pack—follow this method, and you'll be able to improve the operations in one major area of your business rapidly, which will give you the confidence and tools to improve *any* area of your business.

I'm an operations girl, so, naturally, I have a checklist for you. A few of the items may be surprising . . . don't worry, just keep reading and I'll unpack each one:

The 90-day Sabbatical Method Checklist[11]

1. Choose one area of your business that you want to focus on
2. Block off one hour in your calendar at the same time every week
3. Determine the time window for your jumpstart
4. Determine what *type* of sabbatical you're going to start with (you'll find out more about this below)
5. Commit to my 5 daily habits

By the end of this chapter, you'll have everything you need to start your 90-day sabbatical jumpstart.

1: Choose One Area

When my husband and I started our renovation project, we listed off the items we needed to finish in order of importance. At the time, we were living with my parents with a 15-month-old. It was critical that we move in as quickly as possible. Naturally, we

---

[11] Note: You can download this checklist at sabbaticalmethod.com/toolkit.

decided to tackle the bedrooms first. These were low-hanging fruit, which just needed a coat of paint and some carpet, then, *presto*, we were on our way.

Beyond that, we made a list of everything for every room. Prioritizing the list of rooms, and creating a prioritized checklist for each room, which went something like this:

- Demo
- Patch
- Primer
- Paint
- Floor
- Molding
- Paint

By following our moderately detailed plan, we had a beautiful new, upgraded home, nestled in the Pocono Mountains by the time my son was born. Is there still more to do, even to this day? Yes. But is it a night and day improvement from where we were when we began? Also, YES.

In your business, you want to do the same.

Even if you're doing a complete remodel, you want to start with a plan, begin with the demo, then layer everything else on. It doesn't matter what was there before or who may have never cleaned behind their oven or updated their carpets. Just move forward.

Importantly, I want you to find the one area of your business that you want improved, the critical one, in the same way we focused, first, on our bedroom.

- Do you feel rushed, or as if you're reinventing the wheel every time you onboard a new client? Start here.

- How about hiring and training a new team member—do they know where to go to find the resources they need to do their job? If not, maybe you should start here.

Your one area could be increasing revenue, tightening up the performance of your team, revamping your marketing and your brand, or creating a more sustainable work-life balance, or it could be a combination of a few things. The point is to get clear.

We need to viscerally understand where we're going, what we're trying to improve, and why it's critical to our overall mission and vision for how we want to live and impact the world.

So, the first thing on your sabbatical checklist is to begin with one goal. Eventually, as the Sabbatical Method becomes part of your DNA, you can tackle several areas of your business at once. But, for now, focus on one area as you read through this book. That may be optimizing your sales process or equipping your customer support team with training and optimization for how they're handling support tickets. Whatever your one thing is: visualize it.

- What needs to be true in order for this to improve?
- What does the ideal outcome look like?
- How do the people involved feel?
- How do they behave?

To help you determine what area you're going to focus on, take the Operations, Simplified™ assessment at thesabbaticalmethod.com, which will give your business a score for each level, and determine where the gaps are, helping you figure out the best ROI for your efforts.

2: Block One Hour in Your Calendar

In 2004, *Anchorman: The Legend of Ron Burgundy* came out in theaters. At the time, I couldn't get enough of Will Ferrell and the rest of the crew that producer Judd Apatow pulled together for his impressive portfolio in the early 2000s. This particular movie, if you haven't seen it, comically portrays a news team in the 1970s. In the movie, Ron, played by talented Will Farrell, is so dialed into what he's doing when reading the news that he'll read anything that's put on the teleprompter. Anything. I joke with my team that I am Ron Burgundy—put something on my calendar and I will, without hesitance, show up to that thing ready to rock. It's not as comical as Will Farrell, but it ensures that I have the important things carved out in my day.

Take the decision-making out of when you'll focus on your business development by putting what's most important into your calendar. Because, let's face it, if you're reading this now, it's likely that your systems have taken a back seat or fallen to the end of the queue for a little too long.

Make your future self's life easier by blocking out one hour per week (say Mondays or Fridays) to improve the one area of your business you want upgraded. Once that area is improved, you'll have that consistent time on your calendar *already* habitually blocked, allowing you to move to other area(s) of your business. I find that it's helpful to have a consistent time blocked so that you can make sure other team members can be aware of what you're working on and when. If someone else owes you any work or has to give any input or there's any preparation at all, we need to make sure that work is complete before we sit down for those 60 minutes.

3: Determine the Length of Time

I usually take clients on a hard reset for 90 days to get their new Sabbatical Method life on track, which will instill in them some new habits, tools, and tactics. Then, from there, they're able to have a regular cadence that allows them to live the Sabbatical Method life in their business on an ongoing basis.

In this book, I'm going to assume that's what you and I are doing together, as well. For the next 90 days, as you read this, I'm going to help you hard wire for a new mindset. And create a plan to stabilize your business a bit more and improve (at least) that one major area of our business you determine in checklist item number 1.

I *do not* expect most of you to suddenly take 90 radical days off from your business. Some of you may be able to do that, particularly if you're in the corporate world that's paying you to. But for others, we're going to take a different type of sabbatical (keep reading!) . . .

4: Determine Your Type of Sabbatical

There are 3 main types of sabbaticals you can take, and each of them requires you to become someone new for the next 90 days during this initial sabbatical period. Choose 1. This will help guide the decisions you make and how you interact with your team at a high level. If you've never taken significant time off from the business, begin with the first option. If you're a bit more seasoned, feel free to jump out of the business for a bit to balance working on systems and resting exclusively (board member, option C).

A: The Assister

The all-time assists leader for the National Basketball Association is former player John Stockton. He played alongside some of the greatest players of all time including Michael Jordan, Karl Malone, and Magic Johnson.

When he was inducted into the hall of fame in 2009, his career performance stood firmly at the top of the all-time assists records at 15,806.

What may be more impressive than the actual number of assists is that Stockton spent his entire career with the Utah Jazz and each season he was with them (19 total) they made the playoffs. Every single year.

The Assister's role is to do just that, assist. The assist is powerful. And harnessing this in your business is a great way to dip your toes in the water and try removing yourself from day-to-day operations. You won't be responding directly to emails, presenting anything on client calls, tinkering with solutions, or building any products. You'll be assisting others. You'll provide insight and guidance, maybe even a few rules, but you won't be responsible for any of the *doing*.

I challenged a client back in 2019 to only answer his team's questions with screencasts. Here's how it went:

Dave was building web pages day in and day out. He had a small team and was constantly the one who pushed things over the finish line. As part of our work together, I encouraged him to be an Assister for just 2 weeks. Kick everything back to the team, give them guidance and the non-negotiables, but let them do the actual building.

Dave was surprised and delighted that his team stepped up to the plate, and they felt encouraged that he believed in them enough to create final versions of sites and deliver on client calls.

With the information Dave recorded for his team, we built a knowledge base for his team members to reference. Today, Dave focuses solely on selling projects, not on delivering them. And everyone is happier: Dave, his team, and the clients.

Assisting is powerful. Plus, when an owner steps out of their business, it can help identify gaps without pulling the owner out entirely, particularly when the business isn't ready for that yet.

B: The Trainer

Similar to the Assister, the Trainer does not touch any work. They don't answer emails, and they're likely not in the bulk of team meetings. I like to think of the Trainer as Insanity creator and head trainer, Shaun T.

For those of you reading who don't know Shaun T., you're in for a fun ride.

I attended a live Shaun T. training when Insanity was blowing up back in 2010. Shaun T. coincidentally grew up in Deptford, New Jersey, just one town over from where I grew up. He came to our community center one evening to lead a session in the basketball gym. The gym was filled wall to wall with people. Teachers, kids, moms, dads, pretty much everyone in town came out of the woodwork, from all levels of physical fitness to try Insanity.

His program was aptly named, as this routine was challenging. Every single one of us was sweating, breathing hard, and disheveled. It was a great workout.

Though he began his career as a fitness trainer, his core message has evolved into trusting and believing in the power of *transformation.* That's what we do as trainers: we transform something from a crappy "before" state into a better "after" state.

Being a Trainer in your business may look like you leading all-hands meetings or gathering your team to communicate how they can transform their departments or how the goals for the quarter will transform the business. To be clear, you're simply leading them through exercises to think through and giving them examples on how to achieve goals, but you're not following them back home and telling them what to eat. Give them the tools and let them figure out where they need to go next.

Physical trainers have their fingers on the pulse of what's happening. They assess each client's BMI, goals, and overall progress at specific cadences. They also have their clients self-assess by reporting weight, water intake, food intake, duration, and frequency of exercise.

Sabbatical Method Trainers can implement these habits with their team. Allow each of them to track their progress and pull metrics into the company scorecard that you can review at a weekly or monthly cadence.

Moving into the Trainer role during your sabbatical is a healthy way to break old habits of having the team rely on your input for everything. (If this is your chosen role, you'll want to pay special attention to Chapters 7 and 9 when we discuss metrics and decision-making.)

C: The Board Member

Warren Buffett serves as the Chairman and CEO of Berkshire Hathaway, a multinational conglomerate holding company.

Buffett is known for his hands-off approach to management and for trusting the executives he hires to run the businesses under the Berkshire Hathaway umbrella. In fact, Buffett has famously said that he spends only about 6 hours per year on

Berkshire Hathaway business, vowing to focus only on big-picture decisions, giving management power back to his leadership team.

While Buffett is involved in high-level strategic decisions, such as the acquisition of new businesses, he leaves the day-to-day operations of those businesses to their own management teams. He trusts those managers to make the right decisions and to achieve the results that they've identified.

It's clearly working.

Berkshire Hathaway has grown into one of the largest and most successful companies in the world. This style of management in the business has also allowed Buffett to focus on his strengths, such as investing and capital allocation, while leaving the operational details to others. If you've decided to take a full-on, out-of-office sabbatical, that's what you want to be doing: approving only high-level purchases or participating in strategic conversation about overall company direction.

We want to safeguard your involvement (or, rather, lack thereof) in the business so that you can soak in the time you have with your family, focusing on your health and letting the next phases of the business build in your brain.

I have a client and friend, Yuri Elkaim, who's a *New York Times* bestselling author and founder of Healthpreneur. Back in 2018, we met up at an event in Manhattan Beach, California, and I'll never forget something he shared with me over biscuits:

"It's part of my business plan to take a vacation once per quarter. I get my best ideas on vacation."

There have been several studies conducted on the link between vacation and idea generation. One relatively small study conducted by researchers at the University of California, San

Francisco, and published in the *Journal of Environmental Psychology* involved 124 adults who were randomly assigned to either take a 12-day vacation or to stay at home. Before and after the vacation, the participants completed several cognitive tests designed to measure creativity, problem-solving, and attention.

The results of the study showed that the participants who took the vacation scored significantly higher on the creativity and problem-solving tests compared to those who stayed at home. The researchers concluded that the vacation experience may have provided a mental break that allowed for greater cognitive flexibility and idea generation.

Another study, conducted by researchers at Tilburg University in the Netherlands and published in the *Journal of Happiness Studies*, found that people who took vacations reported feeling more creative, focused, and productive upon their return to work.

We're building your business as a way to serve your life, your community, and your family. Not the other way around. Frequently taking breaks, building the sabbatical concept into the ethos of your business, and allowing yourself the space to connect with others, to think, and to rest, will be what sets you apart from your competition.

5: Commit to 5 Daily Habits

I have some daily habits I want you to maintain throughout the next 90 days. These habits will contribute to the success of your sabbatical and help you get out of your own way. Too many founders hold onto simple things like their inbox or reporting for way too long, ruining their chances of letting go.

A) You only get one hour per day to answer emails (and you can't check them first thing in the morning)

Studies show that beginning your day with a routine that focuses on the most important work you need to do (health, wellness, mindset) will help you have an overall more relaxing and more productive day. Right now, it's 5:17am, and writing this is part of my routine.

If I open up my email this early in the morning, I get reactive and I start solving problems. We don't want to do that. We're creators. And if you don't have something you're creating at the moment, you can read further in this book instead of checking email. It'll be worth it.

B) Create a screencast every day

I'll get into the tactics of this in just a moment, but this is another critical habit we want to build. Each day as you're working on your tasks, choose one thing and record your screen while doing it. Some folks tell me that they don't screencast their tasks because they aren't sure who they'd offload them to or because they don't feel the process is fully fleshed out. Both issues are OK—record anyway. Videos will help someone get mostly (if not all the way) there. As SaaS coach Dan Martell says in his *Wall Street Journal*-bestseller, *Buy Back Your Time*:

"80 percent done by someone else is 100 percent freaking awesome."

Record the video, save it, and when you're ready to train someone or offload that task, you can send them the videos and they can work to get things off your plate. Screencast. Every day.

C) Answer questions with documentation

There are 2 phases to this habit. One phase happens before you've made any screen-casting videos for the given question; the second occurs if you do already have a video for it. Let's say that tomorrow someone asks you the following question:

"Hey Paul, I'm prepping an agreement for a new client; what should go inside?"

If you don't have a recording already, then this is a perfect opportunity to use this question as a prompt for your screencast of the day.

Next time someone asks you this question, reply back with the video. Or, even better, reply with the link to where you keep all your videos. This will help the team build the muscle to get answers to their questions without relying on you.

D) Commit to a metric and look at it every day

Yes, look at the same metric each and every day. Weekends, Christmas, every, single, day. This metric should be a critical one that underscores how your business operates, how you make an impact, or reflective of a goal you have. Set a goal and track it relentlessly.

You could track what time you start work. Or how long you spend looking at email. Or how many sales calls your team made the following day, or your daily spend on paid media. Or you could look at a quarterly growth metric or larger goal. I especially encourage looking at a metric around SOPs.

I've tracked mostly the same numbers for the last 5 years. My favorite metric, the one I look at every day, is how quickly we turn around work here at Operations Agency. Underneath that one, I always take a peek at how many internal revisions we needed to get a quality piece of work out.

Simple, impactful. I know that if my team turns around quality work in a shorter amount of time, my clients can use it to save themselves a ton of headaches; they can iterate faster, improve their workflows, and so much more. Those clients are more likely to stay with us and tell their friends and colleagues about us. Suddenly, by tracking and improving that one metric, we're making a growing impact.

Choose a metric. Centralize it for yourself and look at it every day. Alex Hormozi, entrepreneur and owner of acquisition.com, says that looking at one thing consistently every day will help it grow because the brain tries to solve for the variable. If you look at a metric that's constantly underperforming, your brain is hard-wired to figure out that problem. If we do this for 90 days, we'll have 90 chances at problem-solving. Our brains can't help but find ways to improve it.

E) Take care of your body

I'm not a health coach, a fitness trainer, or a nutritionist, nor do I profess to be. And taking care of your body isn't a business-centric operational habit, but hear me out:

When I take care of my physical body, feeding it with the right nutrients, I show up as a more consistent, impactful leader, both in my home and in my business.

I have never achieved anything of significance when I've let my physical health go. Whenever I feel "stuck" or "unmotivated" I usually find that I have not been moving my body, drinking enough water or eating whole, nutritious foods. If it feels uncomfortable to read those words, then that's probably because it's true for you, too.

Every time I set a growth goal in my business, I always, *always* set a health goal alongside it. That could be losing weight or running 3 miles in under 21 minutes, or it could be completing a full split (which I still have never done, but I'm determined!).

A 2020 study published in the *Applied Physiology, Nutrition and Metabolism* publication found that a 15-minute, high intensity interval training (HIIT) session "results in the greatest memory performance in... older adults compared to moderate continuous training or stretching."

If you want to improve your memory, learn new things, and build new skills, physical activity is one hack that can help you get there.

So, make a quick plan and jot down some commitments you have to improve your health in the next 90 days. Even folks who don't currently exercise or are in the best shape of their lives could include something that stretches them.

A few things I would encourage:

- 8 hours of sleep each night
- 3 liters of water each day
- Move your body to the point of sweating every day for at least 30 minutes
- Eat only foods that grow in the ground or have a momma
- Stretch for 15 minutes in the morning and 15 minutes at night

You may already be doing these things. Great. Keep doing them. Challenge yourself to add a goal into one of these categories. This experience will be worthwhile when you ascend to a new level of leadership in your organization and your community.

A Final Note on Personal & Business Health

You'll hear lots from me throughout this book about the importance of both business and personal health. If you follow me on social media[12] or if you know me personally, you already know that I firmly believe that how you do one thing is how you do everything. And if you are lacking personal health, it's likely showing up somewhere else in your business, or your personal relationship, or even your mental health.

We (the founders) are so closely connected to our business that it's often challenging to detangle us from the day-to-day, from the brand itself, from casting vision, creating value for clients, closing deals. So, if you're feeding your body Burger King, where are you feeding your business a metaphorical "Burger King" meal and expecting it to function well?

If you struggle with physical health, start small. Don't think about being in peak health overnight because—guess what—that's not realistic. And you'll likely give up if you jump into the deep end. No one becomes a marathon runner in a day. Instead, they train. We begin where we are and make a plan to tackle the next, larger challenge.

The best training plans for your health and for your business incorporate a few critical elements: consistency, tracking, and rest.

Consistency: *What can we do every day or every week to improve?*

Tracking: *How are we measuring success?*

Rest: *How much time are we giving ourselves to recover?*

---

[12] You can check out my general happenings and check out my cute kids on Instagram @alycaffrey

These are the basics I want you to carry forward as you're weaving in your own personal health goals throughout our time together.

Simply put, the healthier you are, physically and mentally, the better you're going to run your business. Implementing the Sabbatical Method and using it as a strategic growth tool will help you improve the health of your business and give you more time to focus on improving your life outside of work.

Let's get going!

Yours operationally.

Summary:

- Choose one area of your business from which to take a sabbatical. This could be something as small as answering customer support emails. Whatever it is, make it simple.

- Block one hour per week to work on it.

- Make a plan for how long you're going to be attacking this one area of your business (I recommend a 90-day period).

- Decide whether you're going to be an Assister, a Trainer, or a Board Member for the next 90 days, during your jumpstart sabbatical.

- Create one screencast (minimum) every day.

- Commit to looking at least one metric every day.

- Take care of your body. (Everyone can improve in this area in some small way.)

Critical Action:

Write down your sabbatical plan and post it where you can see. If you're stuck on what to include, I have a template at thesabbaticalmethod.com/toolkit.

Create an opportunity

Create an opportunity for someone's life to be changed by the Sabbatical Method. If you're enjoying the contents of this book so far, here's your opportunity to pay it forward. There are so many people who either don't know me, don't know anyone in my community or, frankly, don't even know they need to read these words to enable change in their lives. There are folks out there scared to confront the brutal truth that they need help, that they need a break, and that they need to start addressing how they operate in order to focus on their overall happiness and impact at home and in business.

The simplest way you can create another opportunity for someone is to leave a review for this book.

The quote listed above is from an incredible book written by the profound life coach, Ed Mylett. Ed's dad was an alcoholic who spent most of his adult life in and out of rehab facilities, constantly relapsing and damaging the relationships of his family and friends. Ed tells this story in his book *The Power of One More: The Ultimate Guide to Happiness and Success* and recalls that it was simply one more person who took the time to care about his dad's recovery that ultimately ended up saving his life.

Your review could connect someone who is struggling with the help they need. It could be the 'one more' experience that Ed's dad had. The one that saved him from himself.

If you're reading this now, my ask is that you stop what you're doing, take 60 seconds to pull out your phone, and leave a review on Amazon.

If you know this will help someone specifically, if you have them pictured in your mind's eye, send them your copy when you're finished or drop them a hint.

By now, you know me a bit, you know I love helping entrepreneurs. By reviewing or referring this book, you are my kind of person. You are helping entrepreneurs. And for that, I am grateful.

When you leave your review or help a friend connect with this book, take a quick screenshot and send it to hello@operationsagency.com. I have lots of goodies for those who create opportunities.

To make it super easy, here's a direct link to the spot on Amazon where you can write the review: https://operationsagency.com/sabbaticalmethod-review. Thank you from the bottom of my heart.

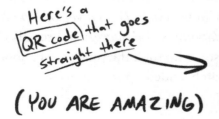

Now back to our regularly scheduled content...

In your corner,

Alyson

CHAPTER 4

OPTIMIZE FOR THE DAY-TO-DAY

Level 1: Part 1, Defining Your Core Processes

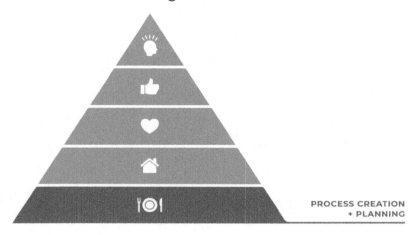

PROCESS CREATION
+ PLANNING

Mission: Enjoy the journey, not just the summit. We're going to walk through the tactics I use to help clients identify what their repeatable daily processes are and how to standardize them. Once your basic systems are standardized, we can assess whether those tasks belong on the founder's plate or somewhere else in the organization

Imagine you want to summit a fourteener in beautiful Colorado. You'd likely pick a day where the weather is nice, and the visibility is clear, so you have the best chance at the best view.

If you're like me, you'd sneak a peek at what it looks like at the top on Google Images (I admittedly do this every single time before I hike anything). And, often, I'll even picture myself there—what it smells like, what the wind feels like on my face. That visualization crystalizes the end goal for me and pulls me through the difficult times on the trail.

If you read any book on vision-casting or goal setting, you've probably received this advice. "Visualize yourself at the end, and you'll have the motivation to press on." I agree wholeheartedly with that advice, and truthfully, there's a ton of research on visualization and its benefits for achieving challenging goals.

But creating a vision helps, only to a point.

When Steve and I were first married, we went on this epic Alaskan Cruise with my cousins, aunts, uncles, and grandparents. It was mid-June and, apparently, the best time of the year to go. We stopped in several locations: Ketchikan, Juneau, Skagway, and Victoria, British Columbia. Steve and I would plan a hike for each location the day before we docked, and as soon as we could get off the ship, we headed straight for the wilderness.

Our third stop, Skagway, had a bit more of an adventurous plan. We'd heard about this crazy trail to an "upper glacial lake," but couldn't find a map that showed the lake. In an effort to not waste any time, my brother (Ryan), Steve, and I just hopped off the ship and headed for the trail.

I'll preface: I gave birth to 2 children without any pain medication. And I will absolutely say that this hike falls firmly into the third-place spot on the list of the hardest things I've ever physically done.

Over approximately 5 miles, we gained over 3,000 feet (about 914.4 m) of elevation over rocky terrain. There wasn't very much break in the trees, so we didn't experience any intermittent stops or lookouts along the way. We'd also seen bear poop pretty early in the hike (we found out later that the trail had been closed midway through our hike due to a bear sighting).

Time was not on our side, either. We had about 8 hours total in Skagway that day, and our hike took about 6 of them. I remember on the way back rushing to ensure we had time to eat a quick fish sandwich and enjoy a cold beer before hopping on the ship.

Admittedly, there were points on the way up that I wanted to stop. And to this day, that experience haunts me somewhat, because I know I was really struggling. You see, when I had our first son, I had no idea what to expect, but the promise of holding my baby at the end made everything worth it; I kind of just went vacant in my own body and got through each contraction one at a time.

But this hike was physically taxing, and I had no idea what I was doing it all for, since we couldn't find images of it online, or even on a map. There was no promise I could imagine, nothing I could see, feel, taste in my mind's eye. There was just rock, a heavy tree line, and (maybe) a bear ready to pick me off.

I was constantly wondering, *Is this worth it?*

Again, this is firmly in the third-place spot for "hardest shit Aly has ever done" list, but you know what? Upper Dewey Lake in Skagway, Alaska is also in the third-place spot for the most beautiful things I've ever seen. (My sons, Frank and John, are tied for first.)

The lake was nestled among glaciers and mountains with water so clear you could see right to the bottom. Around the edges there was a green pasture with beautiful tall pines. The National Park Service runs a small rentable cabin at the top where hikers can reserve and stay the night in this beautiful landscape. It was calm. There weren't many people up there. The terrain had made sure of that.

Turning around, you'd get a peek at the inlet that Skagway is nestled in. The vantage point is over a small waterfall that we heard (but didn't see) on our way up the mountain.

We spent about 20 minutes at the top before time forced us to turn back around and traverse the same path back to the bottom. Rushing to make sure we were back at the ship before it left us in a remote Alaskan town.

With just a quick dopamine hit, a handful of pictures, and some swigs of water, that moment at the lake lasted only a few minutes, and the feeling was fleeting. The intense memories, the feelings, the lessons. . . all came from the *trail*. I remember looking down at the rocky terrain at my feet for hours, getting down on my butt for some portions of the trek just so that I didn't slip and fall, being very careful with my steps so that I didn't get injured. I remember being scared, wondering whether I could do it. It isn't about the view at top; it's about the lessons learned on the path.

Optimizing the Process

Often, in their businesses and their lives, founders spend considerable time looking at the goal, planning the arrival, or casting a vision of what success looks like from the top. That practice will help get you through hard times, absolutely. But if most of our journey is spent on the path, shouldn't we focus on preparing and optimizing for that? Creating mini wins we can celebrate, playing music, taking breaks?

I get it. Entrepreneurs (me included) want [insert thing here] so badly, that we're willing to look right past days, months, and often years of hard work to get there. We always look to what's next, rationalizing away the hardship as just part of the path.

When the world shut down in March of 2020, I remember holding status meetings with all my clients. There was a ton of uncertainty and fear going around. Not just in business, in life as well.

In those first few weeks, no one knew what was going on. Visions were *obliterated.* We didn't know what would happen a year from now: would we be at war? Would half the population be dead? Would we be back at work as normal in 2 weeks?

All we had left was the day-to-day, and the relationships at home.

I spoke with one client who told me he'd not even known his 13-year-old son. He found it challenging to talk with him. They both always had things going on, soccer practice, a business trip, going to a friend's house. Now that was all gone, there were no external factors, no goals to set out ahead.

I know families who went through incredible challenges with mental health and relationships, businesses who needed to let go of every single contract they'd had. The changes were vast. And things were uncertain.

Most plans took unintended turns. I don't know a single person who wasn't affected, in some way, by the events of 2020 and beyond. Visions shifted, changed, or were scrapped altogether.

The companies I know who made things work really well during the pandemic were those with a strong operational foundation and, more importantly, those who were optimized for the day-to-day.

I remember working with a client who trained EMTs for various hospital systems. My team had written many of their SOPs in the years leading up to the pandemic. Their team was small, but they were efficient. And wicked smart.

When the pandemic hit, they realized they had a unique opportunity to distribute Personal Protection Equipment (PPE) and train medical staff on how to use it properly. Providing this additional service didn't even look that different from their day-to-day. Since their operational foundation was solid, they simply applied their practices to another solution.

I've seen companies in manufacturing do this quite often. They have a good facility with solid processes, and they're able to recognize and accept new opportunities simply because their systems are amazing.

Eli Whitney brought us interchangeable parts and mass production back in the late 1700s.

Elements of Henry Ford's assembly line are still used to create cars and other goods to this day.

These 2 obsessed about the process of producing. As a result, they were met with incredible growth opportunities. They optimized the process and ended up with more than they probably ever dreamed of.

Too often we put the goal or the vision as the guiding factor for what we're doing and why we're doing it. Don't get me wrong: vision is important, but the process will be 90 percent of the work.

> Creating a process that's effective and enjoyable will give us all the longevity and the results we need to keep our businesses and our lives intact.

I was listening to an interview once with the legendary course coach, Amy Porterfield. She was recalling her experience and hardship in the early days of launching her programs. She admitted that she'd botched things, fallen short of goals, and was not traditionally successful at the start of her business. But she told me that this saying kept her going: "Just make it one more day."

When she felt as if everything was falling apart, and she wasn't sure what to do next, she focused on the *process*: what she could do today to get her further down the path to where she wanted to go.

I read heartbreaking stories and listened to many interviews of owners who quit too early. They give up because they think they should have arrived already or that they should be hitting targets someone else is hitting. (Social media hasn't exactly helped in this arena.) Many believe they should have achieved what they want by now, so, they quit—the path is longer and rockier than they had originally planned.

But what if we decided to optimize the *path* we're on, instead of just the outcomes? So, here's my challenge: put blinders on to what everyone else is doing and focus on what we can control: our actions and our feelings. *Our process.*

In Ryan Holliday's famous read *The Obstacle Is the Way*, he says this about the will to keep going: "True will is quiet humility, resilience, and flexibility; the other kind of will is weakness disguised by bluster and ambition. See which lasts longer under the hardest of obstacles."

When we focus on the process, we remove our ego. We decouple ourselves from failure. As Holliday also says: "Failure shows us the way—by showing us what isn't the way."

Rocky paths and winding turns are expected. Prepare for them. Optimize the business to withstand and endure challenges. Optimize for the day-to-day. Days bring hardship, unexpected resistance, curveballs, and tantrums. Some days may feel downright impossible. (By the way, these aren't "if's," they are certainties. Steven Pressfield calls this "resistance" in his books *The War of Art* and *Do the Work*.

I've spoken with owner after owner every single week for the last 5 years on my Clarity Calls (our introductory call for prospective clients) who say that they're absolutely burnt out. Sometimes, I joke with my team that we're running a hospital, because everyone comes to us when they have an injury or when something is completely broken or when they're tired and frustrated.

Rarely do folks seek us out to prevent injuries. or work on planning for hardships.

In 2022, we worked with an agency that was having trouble keeping their projects in scope, a very traditional problem that we helped fix. It seemed like a plug-and-play for us. They were a design shop that focused on branding and visual identity. I asked their creative director what he felt the issue was, and he replied, "We need better standards for quality of work." I thought it was simple enough.

But after I did some digging to check out their projects, it became clear that rework was clogging up the system. They had a decent process for delivering work, and it met most of the quality standards we helped them put in place. It just *seemed* like their team wasn't putting out quality work, because a client would request one small edit, and that change would throw everything off pace.

My team decided to optimize their project scope to include rework as part of the design experience. The design agency wanted client input at certain stages anyway, so my team set guidelines and processes to ensure their clients gave better feedback in a shorter timeframe.

The length of their projects decreased by almost 20 percent. It was mind-blowing. They grew their capacity for more projects, and clients were getting faster, more frictionless results. By optimizing for the unexpected, this team found a better way to serve their clients and create a mutual win.

Don't be afraid to look at things objectively and ask yourself, *Is this **genuinely** how we do business?* Often, companies will create a beautiful vision and mission statement, or they'll create the ideal process for clients, but the hard truth is that they're not being real with themselves about how they're actually doing business now.

If that design agency hadn't been real with themselves about the amount of rework they were doing, they wouldn't have optimized the process to handle those requests, and they never would have grown past that obstacle.

So, what's true now about how you're operating? Be real, even if the picture isn't pretty.

If you had to traverse a rocky path up to a glacial lake, would you be prepared? What challenges do you expect, and how can you overcome them with the tools you have now?

We do this in our business all the time: we go out on an epic odyssey, have a detailed destination in mind, but we forget to pack our lunch. We don't optimize for the *experience along the way,* which is how we spend the majority of our days. If you do the challenging work of preparing for the day-in, and day-out, you will create safety in your business, preparing you for the obstacles that lie ahead. You won't be easily rattled when something new comes your way, because you'll have optimized for the day-to-day, allowing you to focus your energy and attention on innovating solutions for the unexpected.

I challenge you to do a sort of state-of-the-union.

Remember: we're on level 1, and we're identifying your core processes.

Standardize Before You Optimize

You need to standardize before you can optimize. It's important to ask yourself, *What are we doing **now**?* not *What do we **want to be doing in the future?*** It's tempting to build a system or write a process for an outcome you want to create, but if it's not accurate, it won't be usable.

Create your processes, then begin to optimize them. Ask yourself and your team: "What would this look like if we did it slightly quicker or at a slightly higher quality? What additions can we bring in? Can we play music, can we add in little celebrations?"

We spend most of the time on the path to our goals, let's define the path and make it worth walking.

Yours operationally.

Summary:
- Standardize your day-to-day processes because you'll spend most of your time doing those things, not celebrating victories at the summit.
- You must standardize before you optimize.
- Create mini wins in the day-to-day.
- Creating effective and enjoyable processes will give you all the longevity and results you need to keep your life and business in-tact.

Critical Action:

At thesabbaticalmethod.com/toolkit, there are 2 exercises to complete for this chapter:

1. My Perfect Week: an assessment of how you spend your time and what brings you energy, joy, and results in your business.

2. The Founder's Matrix: also known as the Zone of Genius exercise by Dan Sullivan. Here, we'll dissect how you spend your week, by segmenting tasks into 4 categories that will allow you to understand the nature of the next hire you need to make.

CHAPTER 5

BECOME A SCREEN-CASTING GOD

Level 1: Part 2, The Art of Knowledge Transfer

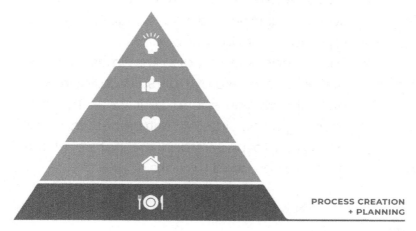

PROCESS CREATION
+ PLANNING

Mission: Get your business out of your brain and into the hands of capable team members. Fold your time creating screencasts of the things you and your team do every day.

In this chapter, we're going to be working that screencast muscle. This is mission critical to getting your business out of your brain. Without a systematic way to create processes we're not going to be able to lean on repeatable outcomes. If we can't access repeatable outcomes and make our business a little more predictable, our dream of longevity and working ourselves out of the business will remain a pipedream.

The good news is that in the digital age, we have an advantage—we can simply record our screen, making knowledge transfer a cinch. Before our modern era, man had 2 traditional methods of transferring knowledge: . . . putting pen to paper and apprenticeships.

Apprenticeships began back in the Middle Ages. Often, apprentices were in contracts for 2-7 years with incredibly rigorous working conditions, 12-hour days, and not much pay. Their knowledge was their payment.

They would spend most of their days shadowing their craftsman, supporting them in their role and taking in all the aspects and moving parts of what the day in the life was for that craftsman.

To complete an apprenticeship, an apprentice would submit their "master craft," at which point they would be judged on their submission, and the teacher would determine whether the apprentice could now become a master craftsman himself. It's no wonder why only a few people were certified master craftsmen. Apprenticeship was a beautiful process, but it sure did take a long time.

Most craftsmen who became masters through the apprenticeship process had to keep their own records and writings around their teachings. So, they were completely immersed in the life of becoming a master craftsman, observing and digesting the information and turning it into written form.

Today, employers can't force their teams to live with them and watch what they do all day, thankfully. We can do better: Thanks to the internet and other digital tools, we can disseminate information to our teams to train them and help refine their skill-sets.

* * *

Let's start with the most basic question: "What the heck should I even be recording?"

When I worked at my first position out of college, I was handed a company handbook. It was a physical compilation of pages in a worn-out binder that hadn't been updated since Moses crossed the Red Sea.

The table of contents had a few hand-written notes in the margins, denoting areas I should be paying particular attention to. Highlighted items included time off requests, company benefits, and 401K contributions. All great things. But none of those helped me do my job immediately.

As an assistant, the items I found most helpful weren't even highlighted—things like how to use the printer, how to open up and shut down the office, etc. These were tasks I completed every day. But those were the *only* daily tasks recorded. Mostly, the book was full of references to obscure items like benefits, or instructions for items that were only needed once a quarter or twice a year. It was bonkers.

When I onboard a new employee, I think about the relationship like this: *How can I use my skills and gifts to be the most useful person to them* **right now?**

For new employees, it doesn't really matter how to request time off, how to contribute to a 401(K), or even (gasp) what the core values are if they can't determine what's expected of them and how to generate results that match those expectations.

Core values, benefits, mission, and vision are all super important, and they should absolutely be written down somewhere for your team to access. But a more important contribution will be creating a bank of accessible procedures that your team can lean on to get results. I'll repeat those last 2 words: get results.

We all want to do a good job. We all want to move the ball forward. Studies show that small, incremental movements in the direction of where we want to go will generate more momentum than waiting to feel inspired.

Jeff Haden says in his actionable read, *The Motivation Myth: How High Achievers Really Set Themselves Up to Win,* "You feel motivated because you took action. Motivation is a result, not a precondition. You don't need motivation to break a sweat. Break a sweat, and you'll feel motivated."

Give your team some action from the gate. Give them something to sink their teeth into.

So, what should you be recording? In short, how you're currently getting results.

If you are your own assistant, project manager, marketing strategist, and salesperson all rolled into one: record how you spend your time getting results in those categories.

Take a look at your calendar, the meetings you've scheduled, the time you've blocked to work on tasks in your business and ask yourself: *Do I have a training on this I could give to someone and get a similar (or at least a meaningful portion of) this result?*

The Traffic Light System

I go through this exercise weekly at Operations Agency, and I encourage my team to as well.

I look at my previous week, the meetings, the tasks, the things I checked off my to-do list. Then I look at what's ahead for the upcoming week: to-do list items, projects, meeting preparatory activities, and I assign each a color. [13]

- **GREEN = delegate.** *This is documented and I could delegate it to someone on my team if I wanted.*
- **YELLOW = document next.** *This is something I should eventually pass off to others on my team, but I don't have any documentation for it yet. (Tasks that are "yellow" could include any that are not documented and range from "I don't love this" to "I really enjoy this." The key is that it's not documented but that it's not driving me crazy.)*
- **RED = document now.** *This task is zapping all my energy, and there's no documentation for it. I need to get it off my plate ASAP by creating a screencast on how to do it.*

This Traffic Light System is the simplest way I have found to get these screencasts knocked out. I start with the RED items, then work my way through the line from there. This exercise will create clarity, offering a constant assessment loop for you (and team members).

This is how I continually exercise my screen-casting muscle. The beauty of this is, that even if you're not going to delegate something today, you will have a walkthrough ready for someone to come in and use when you do want/need to delegate something.

Remember: we're on level 1, and we're trying to get your core processes out of your brain and onto paper.

---

[13] This is much easier once you've completed the Perfect Week exercise from Chapter 4.

A Note on Perfectionism

I'd be silly not to mention the entrepreneurial issue with perfectionism. Here's the one sentence I use to confront this monster:

Do not let perfect be the enemy of done.

Let me ask you this: Would you rather someone come in and help you get 20 percent of a task completed, or would you rather have none of it done?

In the past, you may have tried to delegate and been burned. Maybe someone didn't come back with the results you were looking for, so you decided to jump in and do things yourself because it felt *easier* or *quicker* to do it yourself. Not anymore. We want to change the habits and the health of your business. We want this thing to grow independent of you.

When I taught my oldest son how to brush his teeth, it went in phases. At first, we just built the habit: I brushed his teeth for him each night while he was in the bath.

Next, I handed him the toothbrush at the *end* of the brushing cycle so that he could get used to holding the brush himself and figuring out how to use it. I was still doing the important work, but I was priming him.

Then, I'd let him start brushing, and I'd come in at the end to do a quick pass on all the teeth he'd missed.

Today, I simply applied the toothpaste and handed him the toothbrush. He goes to town.

In this simple example is a truth many owners miss. I get it: We want our team to do everything correctly immediately. But that sets up a false dilemma. We can't duplicate ourselves. No matter how many times we're told we can, it's just not possible. We can, however, be open to the fact that someone may take something and possibly perform it *better* than we can. This is especially true for those YELLOW and RED items on your task list.

Don't let perfectionism hinder your momentum. You can get things off your plate "as is" and then co-create better more efficient ways of doing things alongside your team.

I listened to an audio session from a dude named Steve Chandler back in 2018. It was titled "Expectations versus Agreements." He discusses the rate of success someone has when they feel they have co-created an agreement with someone (a partner, a boss, a friend) rather than simply being expected to do something. In cases of co-created agreements, individuals were completing tasks, meeting deadlines, and holding up their end of the agreement at an 80 percent higher rate than the expectations group.

So, we're actually at an *advantage* if we get a crappy process down on paper that gets results and then we co-create a better version of the process once someone else comes in and gets their bearings.

Co-creating is vulnerable.

You must pull back the curtain, which doesn't feel natural. Most of us want to hide our imperfections, attempting to only put our best work out there. This is particularly true when we have a brand or a business that's really tied to who we are as individuals. Some founders are the face, the name, the everything of the company.

But pulling back the curtain is essential to growth.

So, Let's leverage the tools we have available to us to centralize a knowledge base and transfer that knowledge to our team. To create a business that truly functions independently of us, we need to create a library of resources that our team can visit. They'll be able to check out books on key processes, expectations, and outcomes. This can be *life changing*.

I encourage you not to think of all the things you could document immediately. Like everything worth training for and every muscle worth building, this takes time, consistency, and, you guessed it, *rest*. Start with your own to-do list and go from there.

The simplest way to take massive action is to have a clear list of what needs to be documented and start working bit by bit.

You've got this.

Yours operationally.

Summary:

- Define your documentation list (and have your team do the same).
- Code it with the traffic light system:
  - GREEN= documented, need to delegate
  - YELLOW= to document next
  - RED= to document immediately
- Include the outcomes or results you expect to generate from your activities.
- Don't be afraid to document something that isn't perfect; you can co-create a solution with your team that may be more effective.

Critical Action:

Code your to-do list with the traffic light system. Make sure you always have a clear list of the next 5-10 items that need to be documented. If you reach the end of the list, consider handing this exercise to a team member as well!

CHAPTER 6

YOU ARE YOUR HABITS

Level 2: Build Efficiency and Consistent Improvement

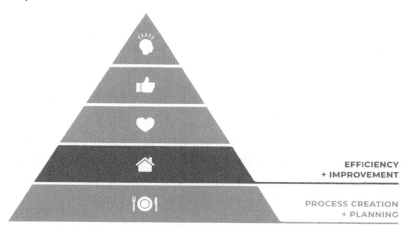

EFFICIENCY
+ IMPROVEMENT

PROCESS CREATION
+ PLANNING

Mission: Define the leading indicators (habits) that make your business operate smoothly and allow you to fall back in love with your workday.

Habits are the most critical piece of development in your business and in your life. I've met so many people who have huge goals and want to achieve big things in life, but have no repeatable, implementable habits that will take them there.

There are a few key ways to influence these habits that will further you along the path toward your goals. The next big thing that influences habits at scale is removing as many decisions from your day as possible and only focusing on making the ones that matter, where to find the data and how to position that. (We'll talk about decisions more in Chapter 9).

Remember when I told you about my previous life of carelessness, excessive drinking, overspending, and generally unhealthy lifestyle choices? Imagine if I had been doing that in my current business—filling it with activities that hinder it from running smoothly, hanging out with the wrong people, and failing to enlist the right help?

That's what many founders are doing right now. They just don't want to face the music.

If you set an audacious goal that requires your company to operate at peak performance but fail to contribute to the health of your business, don't be perplexed in December when you see your annual review and it falls short of your plans.

Companies often come to me to help plan their year and ask me for tips related to goal-setting. I tell them the same thing every, single time: "Instead of planning goals, why don't we plan habits?"

Companies can use projections, forecasting, and models that have worked for other companies to do things like set revenue goals. But the real question to ask yourself is this: *What would I need to do every single day to make this happen? What are the habits I need to build to strengthen my chances of hitting this goal?*

I remember I really wanted to hit $1 million in my second year in business. I was trending well and experiencing great growth, but what an idiot I was. I did the math, which showed that I only needed to close 12 new clients per month to hit that number. *OK, cool,* I thought. *I can do that.*

I quickly realized that I had nowhere close to the number of sales calls I'd need to close that amount of business, nor nowhere near the amount of earned media opportunities to grow my following and my community to generate that many leads. My goal was totally off base.

But starting with *habits* has helped me crush my revenue goal every year since, even if I've toned down my now more modest revenue goals. Plus, I have 3 other elements to show for my habits:

1. I love my workday. Seriously. Each day I do many tasks that I really enjoy doing.
2. My margins are good. I'm not grinding to the bone to take home a mere 3 percent.
3. My team enjoys working with me. By 2023, I've already been around for 5 years, and I have multiple people on my leadership team (and even overseas contractors) who have been with me for 3+ years. Building clear habits and repeatable processes has really helped clarify expectations with my team, so they stick around longer.

How to 3X Your Close Rate

I had a client come to me once with a sales problem. He was attempting to train a new salesperson to take over closing new business for him. He was exhausted and frustrated, because he was closing much more business than the new person was, and he was beginning to wonder whether training a new sales team member was worth the loss of time and money it took to train them. On one of our coaching calls, he told me—through extreme frustration—that he wanted to stop letting this person handle calls because their close rate wasn't great, and he wasn't sure what to do. I asked a quick clarifying question: "Why do you think this rep's close rate has stayed so low?" He paused for a minute. "Because they're not me," he eventually said, adding in a chuckle.

"How can we give your clients more 'you,' but still allow the rep to do the bulk of the work?" I asked.

His wheels began to turn. We decided to implement a simple leading activity to his sales process that included him reaching out to the prospect (with a simple automated email) thanking them for booking a call with his team. Importantly, this message told the prospect that they'd be in great hands.

I encouraged him to stop focusing on the outcome (his close rate) and start focusing on the leading indicators of what creates a good close rate. After implementing that simple email, confidence and trust in the salesperson soared.

A simple templated email from the founder took that rep's close rate from 12 to 20 percent. But we did not stop there.

We looked at some other habits we could build. I asked my client if he did ongoing sales training. "Sometimes," he said. I mentioned we needed to make this a habit. So, my client and his sales team member got on a call every morning for 15 minutes to address the calls for the day. On these calls, my client gave his salesperson deep, experienced insights into their market, among other sales tactics, such as objection-handling. They did this every weekday.

After just 30 days of implementing this daily sales huddle, the representative's close percentage jumped from 20 to 40 percent. He closed double the clients. That's lunacy!

But it's not the results that are important. Sure, I'm happy that this salesperson was able to increase their close rate and that the founder could step back from sales calls. However, the real

value comes from now having a *process* to train new sales team members, along with having a leading indicator my client knows will work. (As a bonus, they co-created some of the process together!)

Now, my client doesn't need to reinvent the wheel and throw things up against the wall to see what sticks. Instead, he knows what he needs to do, the plays he needs to run, and he can tweak the process as the company grows.

Habits don't need to last forever, but they can help set us up to achieve outcomes. Business habits also allow us to make better forecasts and create better goals for our business. If we set our goals by reverse-engineering our habits instead of the other way around, we are much more likely to keep those commitments and achieve our goals.

***

Will Durant and his wife spent more than 40 years writing *The Story of Civilization,* an 11-volume work that discusses the entire historical, human experience. For one volume, 10, the series won a Pulitzer Prize. What was Durant's secret to success?

"We are what we repeatedly do. Excellence, then, is not an act, but a habit."[14]

Will Durant understood that being excellent is having excellent habits. Instead of striving for excellence by pulling an all-nighter, why not build a daily or weekly habit to contribute to that outcome?

We create so much more confidence when we build on habits, versus tackling something overnight. The chances to iterate

---

[14] *The Story of Philosophy* by Will Durant

are much greater when we repeat a task, and we become better people when we implement better habits.

You can spend your days doing things you love doing by forming healthy habits, which increase positive outcomes in your business. Fall in love with the *process* of achieving your goals. Fall in love with the *habits* that create the outcomes you desire.

Start by Doing Everything

A mentor once told me: "Do *everything* in your business before you offload it."

I thought that was odd. I thought surely, I would never be responsible for coding anything on my website, because I just didn't have the skills. You may be thinking the same thing: some things just fall outside the founder's expertise.

What I applied from that advice was to at least understand the process before offloading it to someone. Back in 2019, I was managing our website when something went down just after I'd landed one of the biggest media gigs we'd had up until that point. The person who built my site hadn't given me the processes for how to troubleshoot the website when something breaks.

I watched 4 to 5 hours of videos on YouTube before changing the code on our WordPress site.

Needless to say, I now understand the process.

This frustrating experience prompted me to learn about what my website needed in terms of basic care, every single month. As I got deeper and deeper into solving the problem, I realized other areas that needed updating, saw that our apps were out of date, . . . it was all a mess. I was clearly missing an important habit in my business.

A few weeks later, I called my friend, Mike, to help me create a new and better functioning site. He manages it every month to this day.

Understanding the basic outcomes you're looking to achieve will help you define your critical habits.

Remember: we're on level 2 trying to establish habits. Habits create consistency. Consistent businesses are more predictable and more scalable.

The 3 Elements of Every Healthy Habit

Building healthy habits for our business (and our life) comes down to 3 critical elements.

First, we need to identify what those even are.

If I want to lose weight, a healthy habit I can keep could be as simple as not eating after 8pm or going for a 30-minute outdoor walk each day.

Second, we need to set ourselves up to track progress and effectiveness (something we'll dive deeper into in the next chapter).

Sticking with the losing weight example, I may find that restricting meals and walking simply aren't making much progress toward my goal. I may need to implement additional habits.

Third, we need to be iterative. The first set of habits, the first schedule, the first goal you put out there may not be the one. And that's OK. We're not here to make excuses for why we can't do things. However, if you implement a new workout plan and you're so sore to the point where you can't walk, guess what? That pain is going to stall your overall momentum since it'll be twice as hard now to get up and do tomorrow's workout.

Push yourself to be just 1 percent better each day. Generating momentum is the number-one way to motivate yourself, your team, and your business. Once you have some momentum, you can always double down.

First, look at your goals. Look at your vision. Every outcome we achieve in life and business has leading indications of success. Simply put, habits. When I start to reverse-engineer my results, I ask 3 critical questions…

1. **What are the current habits contributing to those results?**
    Where are we spending our time and money on generating new business, developing the product, marketing the product. We need to define each habit before we can optimize it. If we know what the current habits are that achieving desired results, then we can work on answering the second question.

2. **Do the current habits generate *consistent* results?**
    If you're reaching out to 10 new podcasts per week to be featured in the media, and it generates 2 bookings on average, that's a good leading indicator that drives results. Once we know the input metrics are working, we can move forward and address other indicators in the process, such as calls to action.

    Consistency is a big fish. To discover whether you're executing on this, you may need to think through where you're housing critical data. For simplicity's sake, I usually recommend starting with keeping a log in a simple spreadsheet.

3. **Are there any habits (tasks) that only the founder or another senior leader knows how to do?**

If you answer yes to the above question, please visit Chapter 2 to go through the exercise of getting these habits recorded, documented, and primed, so you can invite someone else into the business to help generate results at a higher level.

Remember: if you are still the only one driving most of the results, everyone is looking to you to lead by example. Jump in, develop healthy habits, document them, and show your team how to handle these, and document *their* tasks.

Habits in Every Area of Business

I typically break product and service businesses down into a few buckets of healthy activities.

- **#Marketing**: How are we generating new followers, driving free value, more eyeballs, and potential customers?
- **#Sales**: How are we converting new followers and eyeballs into paying customers?
- **#Fulfillment**: (For service businesses) How are we keeping the promises that we make to clients?
- **#Product**: (For product businesses) How are we keeping our promises with our product development and delivery?
- **#Operations**: What people, systems, and processes do we have in place to achieve our revenue goals?
- **#Finance**: How do we use and manage our money to accelerate our growth?

This isn't a comprehensive list, but it should get you started! Go get those new healthy habits.

***

Creating habits in our business is critical to building a healthy, predictable, and sustainable operation. Your business organization works the same as a human organism—crap in, crap out. We want to make sure we're not feeding our business junk food or forgetting to exercise. If we want to create an entity that functions independent of us, we must help define its basic leading metrics so that we can understand how it needs to behave to achieve the results we want.

Understanding these habits is the first step to defining a business that can function without any one person.

Yours operationally.

Summary:

- Your business has habits that must be completed every day to achieve your goals.

- If those habits don't exist, or aren't clearly defined, you will fall victim to the urgent fires that crop up.

- Always start by defining your current (healthy) habits. Next, think through what outcomes they impact, then determine whether those habits are documented so they can be trained and leveraged at scale.

- Remember: If you're currently tied to most of the results in your business, most of the habits that must be scaled must start with you. Set an example for your team and develop healthy habits. Lead by example.

Critical Action:

Define one leading indicator for each of the core functions of your business. (I also call these "core processes.") This one leading indicator must be essential and must drive results.

Example of a leading indicator for #Marketing: reach out to 10 new podcast features per week.

Core functions:

#Marketing

#Sales

#Fulfillment (service businesses)

#Product (product businesses)

#Operations

#Finance

CHAPTER 7

LET'S GET READY FOR METRICS!

Level 3: The Leading Indicators

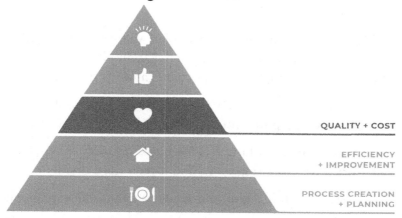

QUALITY + COST

EFFICIENCY
+ IMPROVEMENT

PROCESS CREATION
+ PLANNING

Mission: Define which metrics in your business yield the highest outcomes and how you can strategically place metrics to implement a feedback loop at scale. You can't improve what you don't measure. Let's get to it.

Michael Buffer, the famous voice behind "LET'S GET READY TO RUMBLE!" makes between $25,000-$100,00 every time he says those words in a crowded arena. He's reportedly been paid $1 million for one gig. Why? Because of the outcome it creates.

This phrase was distilled, improved, habitual-ized, tracked, and valued over the years of Michael Buffer's career. Some suggest that he's generated $400 million in licensing fees alone.

Michael started using the phrase to begin matches in 1984. It gained massive popularity, so he decided to trademark it back in 1992. He's been a huge influence on boxer Sugar Ray Leonard, who once told Buffer: "When you introduce a fighter, it makes him want to fight."

These words, said in this particular way, have an incredible effect on fighters, and the crowds in the arena. It's not fancy. It's not complex. It's simple, it's repeatable, and it's trackable.

Michael has become an icon in the boxing and fighting world because he's pinpointed this major benefit to his craft.

This is the power of impact, the power of metrics. We know what works, we put a ring on it, and it pays huge dividends.

I worked with a digital marketing agency a few years ago whose finances were an absolute mess. My team had no idea when we sat down to work on their project what we were going to encounter.

My client had no idea what their gross profit margins were on their projects, how much it cost them to acquire a customer, or how long, on average, clients stayed customers—all important numbers to know if you're running an agency.

Messy metrics meant messy outcomes for my client. Their internal team was unclear what the turnaround times were, what results were expected and how they could help clients win.

We did an operational audit with them and quickly discovered that it took them over 2 months to onboard a new client. Two months. Then, with a little more digging, we found that their average retention rate was only 3.5 months on average, probably due in large part to the length of the onboarding time.

I sat down with the owner to understand why this was all happening. He mentioned that clients take too long to get back to them with the information they need to set up their account (they worked with Google Ads and reviews).

I had him walk me through his current onboarding process. Not once did they get on an administrative call with clients to check all the boxes for onboarding. We implemented that the following week. Over the next 30 days, client onboarding time-line on average dropped down to 2 weeks—a decrease of 75 percent. That means less cost for my client and less frustration all around. My client was thrilled.

I also helped them make some rules of engagement (standards) around setting up, maintaining, and managing projects. Soon, their team was able to pinpoint issues in the client journey and figure out how to get their clients faster results. Today, my client has retained their customer load for an average of 9 months, and their client results have gone through the roof.

Measuring what matters is critical to making some of these key upgrades in your workflow. It could end up bringing in more revenue and more overall profit like it did with my client.

In the previous chapters, we've already discussed tracking and measuring (at least) one vital metric every day. In this chapter, we're going to take that idea and run with it—discovering all the key metrics you should be tracking in your organization.

What to Measure

First, ask yourself, *What is my customer's (or client's) journey?*

There are plenty of fun and helpful resources on developing a killer client journey, but first, we need to start where we are and figure out one simple thing: *What work am I doing to keep the promises we're making to customers?*

Ultimately, we can shave dollars off customer acquisition costs or find more efficient ways to close new business, but in my experience the quickest way to pad the bottom line isn't by getting *more* customers. *Gasp*! It's by being more intentional about the ones you already have.

So many entrepreneurs churn and burn through customers and clients all in an attempt to grow. They chock up cancellations, refunds, and chargebacks to "lessons," continuing to focus on acquiring new customers, often with one-off or off-process projects.

I had an owner come to me just a few weeks ago telling me that his chargeback rates were through the roof. Clients were canceling left and right, because his media buying team had no idea what outcomes they were aiming for, and no idea of the expected cadence for updating accounts. He was pissed (which is a pretty big understatement).

Getting clear on the current client journey can help us identify a few things: How long does it take us to get our client their first win? What are the results they can expect, in what order, and on what timeline?

I'd be remiss to write a book about operations and not talk about McDonald's, right?

If you haven't heard the origin story, I'll summarize: Ray Kroc stumbled upon this well-oiled machine of a business run by Dick and Mac McDonald in 1954. Kroc was amazed, not so much by the creativity or ingenuity of the McDonalds, but by the reliability of their system. Each time he went to the restaurant, he had a burger in minutes. The brothers' store also only sold burgers, shakes, and fries. Nothing else.

After a tour of their small kitchen, Kroc realizes that the Speedee Service System (their process) was the key behind the delivery of their products.

He reportedly drew the system out for every single franchise to follow and would run drills with the team. Each part of the system was meticulously timed to meet expectations. [15]

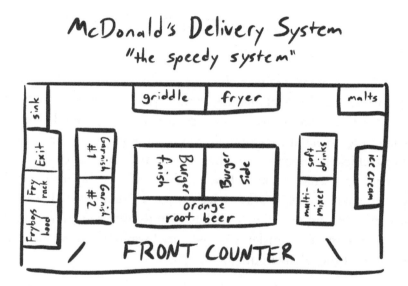

McDonald's kitchens are notoriously small. The Speedee Service System was responsible not only for McDonald's quick, consistent, and quality service, it was also responsible for increasing their profits on real estate. With a clear system and measurable, trackable metrics that led to results (timeliness), staff

---

[15] If you haven't heard all the ins and outs of the McDonald's story, watch *The Founder*, a docudrama starring Michael Keaton. It's a fascinating rise to power.

simply needed less space to operate. Eventually, all this became the foundation for Kroc's Hamburger U, a training program launched in 1961 to teach McDonald's franchise owners how to operate well.

McDonald's Speedee Service System is incredible for so many reasons: repeatability, scalability, teachability. But the real secret, in my opinion, is their consistency. They deliver on promised results consistently and *rapidly.*

I went to Shanghai for a short human resources internship when I was in college. It was fascinating to see a Chinese city and work in the engineering facilities at Johnson Matthey, a company my father has worked with for over 40 years.

When my father and I checked into the Marriott, there was a Starbucks and a McDonald's at the base of the hotel. My dad and I, jetlagged and unsure of what time it was, decided to grab something to eat at McDonald's. I got a double cheeseburger and some chicken nuggets with their sweet and sour sauce—something I have enjoyed since I was a child. What I bit into tasted exactly like home. It was exactly what I'd expected. I wasn't standing in line reading the (albeit slightly different) menu and waiting to place my order. I knew what I wanted, I went there to get it, and they delivered.

As owners, we try so hard to deliver an exceptional experience and we often end up missing the opportunity to simply *deliver.*

If that statement is disconcerting to you, then you probably need to re-read it.

It's often better to deliver an experience that's consistent rather than excellent half the time and mediocre on the other half. It sends mixed messages to clients and customers and, ultimately, they begin to lose trust. The saying "under promise, over deliver" is one of the best pieces of business advice out there. But, if you can't over deliver, at least *deliver.*

Where Are Customers Falling Off?

The next thing you want to determine in your client or customer journey is where people are falling off (particularly true for service-oriented companies). How many times on average does someone return to purchase your product? How long are they keeping your subscription active or their retainer intact? These answers will give us so much information about delivery performance.

The goal should always be to keep a client for one more month. What would you need to do, what systems would you need to implement, what support would your customers need to receive from you to stay for just *one more month*?

If your clients are getting fast, consistent results with you, there shouldn't be any reason for them to cancel or not return, unless the issue is quality, which we'll discuss in the next chapter.

Remember: we're on level 3 adding a tracking mechanism for the way we deliver our products and services.

Regular Check-ins

A well-placed report or check-in can do wonders. Plus, these can even offer to show your client what's next in your journey—an upsell, cross-sell, or a way to work deeper with you and your team.

We worked with a web agency back in 2020, a company that builds websites and runs Google Ads for churches so that they can impact the lives of their congregations and communities.

When the world shut down, so did in-person worship. It was challenging for religious institutions to reach their congregations. Our client, the web agency, suddenly became instrumental in helping churches pivot to online services during the pandemic.

Interestingly, the upheaval brought with it an opportunity— because churches had to move online, the web agency was able to help them see where people were falling off the "customer journey," how many services congregants attended. and over what period of time. This information told church leaders which online activities were serving families with children, which were hitting home with the whole congregation, and which days and times were most watched. All this information allowed the church to better serve their congregations.

With my client, I discussed adding in a screencast overview for pastors to review the performance of their website each month, including which sessions were most heavily attended and what the general growth of their following was. (An insight that's only helpful because my client was already capturing and tracking the data!)

My client also provides content marketing services to Christian nonprofits, a logical next step to providing added value to their customers. So, after diving in together, my client and I found the website reports to be the perfect place to make suggestions about content, providing the next step in their client journey.

See how simple that all was? Your customers want results, and they want to be led. Lead them.

***

If you're looking for repeatability, scalability, and reliability, creating core processes and measurables around them are absolute non-negotiables. Metrics allow you to keep tabs on how things are going with your customers, enabling you to spot red flags earlier, know if you need to make changes to offerings, add more resources, or pivot your services altogether.

And if you're looking to manage your business from a "board member" sabbatical position (see Chapter 3), then metrics that follow the customer journey will bring clarity and decrease stress, both for you and your team.

Let's get ready for metrics!

Yours operationally.

Summary:

- Create metrics that measure key outcomes in your business.

- Looking at metrics consistently will help you deter-mine where to tweak things as you're growing your business or handing things off to others.

- Be objective. Let your metrics tell you how to operate, so that you can focus on the why.

Critical Action:

Create your company scorecard. Define a handful of metrics (I usually choose 3-5 in each department) and then commit to filling this out every week. You can do it a few times, then have your assistant take over.

Remember, if you need some support, all the resources, training videos and templates are downloadable for free at thesabbaticalmethod-book.com/toolkit.

CHAPTER 8

CLASSIC COCA-COLA QUALITY

Level 4: Mastering Growth with Quality and Cost

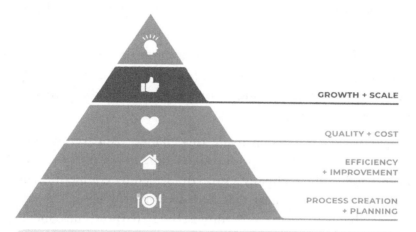

GROWTH + SCALE

QUALITY + COST

EFFICIENCY
+ IMPROVEMENT

PROCESS CREATION
+ PLANNING

Mission: To place your business right in the cross hairs of quality and cost. Once you understand your marketplace positioning for all your products and services, you can have a better understanding of how you must structure your operations for scale.

In the spring of 1985, the Coca-Cola company made one of the biggest mistakes in product history. They launched new Coke.

They were changing their secret formula for Coke. In the opinion of leadership, they were "upgrading" the flavor. After 200,000 taste-tests confirming that customers preferred the new recipe, new Coke hit the market.

Consumers panicked. They bought thousands of dollars' worth of Coke and stuffed it into their basement, preparing for an apocalypse. People protested, wrote letters to the board, and were unmistakably loud about their opinion that new Coke was not for them.

In June 1985, they'd receive an average of 1,500 phone calls per day to their 800-GET-COKE hotline complaining about the new recipe and requesting (more likely, demanding) that old Coke be returned.

Why had leadership made this change? Apparently, Coke sales had stagnated, and prior to launching new Coke, there had been a lull in the company's growth, driven by competition and lack of brand awareness that had declined for about 15 years prior. This new recipe was supposed to energize sales and the brand.

New Coke lasted only 79 days before enough backlash occurred for the company to rethink new Coke, eventually bringing back the old recipe, calling it Coca-Cola Classic. Whether this was the most expensive marketing stunt in history or the most epic product failure of all time, we'll never know.

But the lesson to take from the new Coke failure is that sometimes new is not the answer. I'm even talking about new growth and new customers.

New Is Not Always the Answer

New Coke fundamentally failed because it was focused on generating *new* consumers and not enough focus was on the loyal customers—the dedicated fans who, in the summer of 1985, were buying cases of Coca-Cola and hoarding it in their basements and pantries.

Coca Cola didn't need new customers. They just needed to listen to their current ones.

Founders forget this truth all the time. A market goes stale, we don't see the growth that we're thinking, and we decide to launch something new, create a new revenue stream, break into a new market. Instead, we should be obsessing over the quality of what we're already doing, better-serving the people who have been with us for—in Coke's case—decades.

The old adage, "quality over quantity," is incredibly powerful, and it helps us be more predictable operationally.

This will also positively impact our bottom line. Reports show that consumers who have already purchased your product or service are 60 to 70 percent more likely to purchase again if they have a quality experience.

Thousands of software companies take advantage of this every year when they launch discounts on annual plans, which is particularly attractive for current customers, offering them more of what they already want, at a discounted rate. As an added bonus, this creates some additional upfront cash flow for the business. It's an all-around win.

In my experience, businesses suffer quality issues for a few reasons:

- **They grow too quickly.** They can't create the same outcomes for customers at scale. This is a huge issue operationally because it'll cause an expansion and then a retraction, perhaps even leading to hiring new employees, buying new equipment, and purchasing new software, then needing to cut back shortly thereafter.

This sudden retraction can also damage brands, leading to a lack of trust in the marketplace.

- **They don't have quality control measures in place.** There's not a dedicated member of the organization (or a team of people) making sure that the deliverables for clients and customers are aligned with their measures of quality. Or, more often than not, those measures don't exist. Especially for service providers, this is tough at scale. If there aren't standards in place for how experiences are delivered, it'll always be a subjective conversation with clients and with employees. Performance will likely be inconsistent and challenging to predict.

- **They don't talk to their customers.** Simply asking customers what they want, how they are experiencing the brand and how they feel working with you is improving their life is a great way to gauge quality and longevity of a customer relationship. It'll create the feedback loop you need to create or improve measures of quality, product features, and overall customer experience. If the Coca-Cola Company had done this before launching 'new Coke' they'd likely saved millions.

I'm not suggesting we limit our potential impact by refusing to launch new products into the market. But let's make sure we don't scrap what's working and the opportunity to make a greater impact with what we're *already* doing.

Remember: we're on level 4 priming the quality of our solutions for growth.

Improve Other Areas Besides Quality

You don't always need to improve quality. You could also find new ways to provide the same quality outcome for a cheaper price. Just look at Walmart.

Walmart's main marketing differentiator is that their products cost less than their competitors'. A report from Clark in 2018 found that Walmart's prices were on average 34 percent lower than Amazon's.

Walmart does a fantastic job keeping their operating costs low so they can pass on those savings to their customers. They hire employees at minimum wage and give them process-driven training. Their store design is minimal and new locations can be built quickly. Even one of Walmart's largest competitors, Target, has begun building 'mini-stores' to capitalize on the benefits of a location becoming operational as quickly as possible.

Now, there's an important intersection here that must be discussed: quality and cost control go hand in hand.

Let's just say, for the sake of argument, that new Coke was an incredible marketing scheme to revitalize the relationship with its current customer base (sort of like when you threaten to take your kiddo's favorite toy away if they don't do X).

Once leadership even mentioned that consumers would be losing the traditional beverage, Coke's loyal fans snapped into action. They bought a ton of products and made an enormous amount of noise, creating a ton of publicity around Coca-Cola Classic and their original recipe.

The Coca-Cola company leadership team may have known that this expensive scheme would cause the marketplace stir that it did. Perhaps they were betting that people would panic, believing that if Coca-Cola Classic were no longer accessible, life as we know it would be over, and the country would lose an invaluable piece of American history, and childhood memories, along with the identity of a nation, would suddenly be gone.

What if you understood your customers that deeply? There's immense power in knowing, intimately, where quality and cost intersects at your company:

- How much do you need to spend to create a new customer versus keep a current one?
- When you do create a new customer, how long do they stay with you?
- How much do they spend on average?

Knowing these numbers can help you make some of the most important decisions you will need to make in your business (we'll cover decision-making in Chapter 9). It likely helped the Coca-Cola Company. And it certainly has helped retailers like Walmart price their products, order inventory and create a surprisingly efficient supply-chain management system.

Staying in the crosshairs of quality and cost can help you determine your operating aim. What are you really looking to hit, and are your other operating functions acting for or against this target?

I help companies determine this by looking at a few key factors:

1. Time: how quickly does your market expect you to turn this around?
2. Money: how many resources does your market have to solve this problem?

Now, these aren't the only factors that your customers are considering, but they are likely the first 2.

We can easily chart these into a grid to consider how your operating costs and overall complexity must meet your market and the promises you're making to them. I'll break delivery down into 4 key distinctions and place them on an axis.

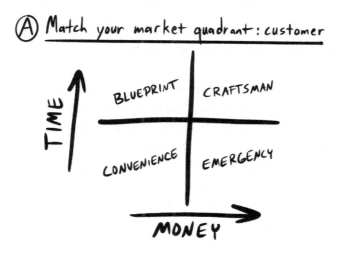

(A) Match your market quadrant: customer

BLUEPRINT | CRAFTSMAN

CONVENIENCE | EMERGENCY

TIME

MONEY

In the top right you have customers with an abundance of time and money. I call this the "craftsman" quadrant. Here, customers have time, they have a large budget, and they want things not only done right, but per their own specifications. Custom home-builders, high-end web designers, and the like are servicing these customers. In my experience, this is where most service providers live in the beginning of their business. They have a skill, they provide it for (hopefully) a high-watermark, high-profit price, and can only work with a select few clients at a time.

In the top left, you have customers who have plenty of time, but little money. These are commonly "blueprint" buyers, or people who can get things done themselves with a little help. If you have a product or service that can help them understand your process, you can usually offer information products at this level and let customers take the results into their own hands.

These should be high-value and high-profit but require little to no time from anyone on your team. Walmart has firmly placed itself in this category. Their stores are sprawling, and they optimize their shopping experience for people who have budgets and the time to walk through and shop the deals in a variety of categories.

In the bottom left, you have customers with no time and no money. These are your "convenience" customers. They want something that will work today that they can toss in the trash tomorrow. Single-use folks. Think of walking into a convenience store, grabbing a coffee from the counter, paying quickly, and getting back into your car. Marketers sometimes call these folks "tire-kickers." My opinion: convenience customers likely *do* have time and money to spend, just not on solving the problem that you specifically solve. They're spending their time and money elsewhere. If we meet them where they are, at the convenience store, they'll purchase $3 coffees in toss-away cups from us 6 days per week for the rest of their lives, and be pleased doing it. These solutions should be low-cost and incredibly process-driven and able to be offered at scale as soon as possible.

In the top left, you'll find your most motivated customers. Those with no time and an abundance of money. They have an emergency, and they are ready to pay to solve their problem. Their solutions need to be quality, but they also need to happen quickly. This is where quality and cost come to the most interesting intersection. Many businesses stay firmly planted in one of the other quadrants and we rarely see someone dominate in the speed and high-ticket category. Afterall, expensive, fancy things take time. But if you can operate like a high-end hospital, you have the opportunity to bring home a good profit margin and change people's lives.

Ⓑ Match your market quadrant: Ops quality

TIME

THE ARCHITECT

THE CUSTOM HOME BUILDER

THE STORE CLERK

THE ER DOC

MONEY

Charting each of your products and services in one of these quadrants will help you determine what level of pricing to offer to your market and what level of quality they expect. Say your child breaks their arm and you take them to the emergency room. If the doctor came out with crumbs on his shirt and said that he'll fix the arm next Tuesday, you'd be livid, and never return.

Businesses who operate really well understand where they are planted in this grid and fulfill the expectations of their customers while keeping their costs under control. They use it as a guideline for making decisions about adding costs, steps, and team members. (And to assess assets as well).

Wheels Up 360 is commonly referred to as the Uber of the skies. They were founded in 2013 to give individuals and businesses a way to access frictionless air travel solutions. Their membership includes over 1,500 private planes varying in size and amenities. This innovative brand makes flying private more accessible to those who can't afford their own plane or to staff a team to maintain it. It's a genius idea. They realized an affluent and underserved market and knocked it out of the park.

Since the COVID-19 pandemic, private jet companies have been steadily increasing their member base. Wheels Up announced a record quarter in Q4 of 2022 in a steadily decreasing economic market. People were still joining this exclusive community and booking chartered flights during a recession and looming market collapse.

They reported 12,661 active members by the start of 2023, each of whom pays at least $3,000 in annual membership fees, plus the cost of their charters. The average revenue per flight is just north of $14,000. And they're growing. Year over year.

Wheels Up 360, a $1.6 billion privately owned company, knows where they stand: delivering high quality at a high cost, and they're firmly positioned in the bottom right quadrant. They only serve folks who have substantial amounts of money and very little time. They are now one of the largest private charter companies in the world.

Do What You Do Really Well

We want to look at our solution and understand where it falls in the grid. It'll help us determine what kind of gusto our operating procedures need to have to pull things off, both in quality and in cost.

My goal is to always begin simple, with the non-negotiables, and then add on as we get better at doing the basic things really well.

Designing your business to operate well and serve your customers' needs won't leave you with a leaky fulfillment system or put your business at risk for dumping too much money into operating costs. If we can optimize what we're already doing and improve upon serving the market we already serve, we can achieve faster and more accurate results.

Use these concepts as guiding measures for making decisions at scale. Want to implement a fancy new software, develop an app, code a new feature, launch a new product or service line? Start here. Ask yourself if you have the budget and if your ideal customers expect this to be part of the experience. This won't be the end-all-be-all final point of your decision-making, but it'll give you a good baseline for what's important and what's, well, extra.

Give 'em Classic Coca-Cola quality!

Yours operationally.

Summary:

- If it isn't broken, don't try to fix it. If your solution is working and selling like hotcakes, don't launch New Coke.

- Businesses suffer quality issues because they don't understand where they fall in the delivery matrix.

- Charting your product or service delivery in one of the 4 quadrants will help you determine best practices for quality and cost.

- Creating a clear guiding measure will help you make important decisions at scale.

Critical Action:

For each product and service you offer, chart it on this grid. The goal is to understand at a high level where your costs and complexity need to be to pull off your solutions at scale. You can watch the full video training and snag the worksheet in the Toolkit at

sabbaticalmethod.com/toolkit

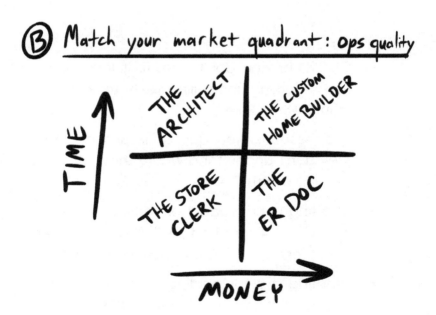

CHAPTER 9

MASTER DECISION-MAKING

Level 5: How to Profit and Prosper

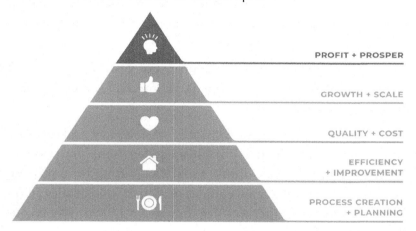

Mission: Determine what essential items need our attention and what can really improve our life and our business.

The Process of Decision-Making Matters

Every week I listen to this incredible podcast called *Family Brand*. It's amazing. The hosts, Chris Smith and his wife, Melissa, have a program for entrepreneurial families that helps them create a brand for their family and unite together under a shared mission. Their content is insightful, caring, and super interesting.

Anyone reading this with children should absolutely go check it out.

A few months ago, they had marriage experts on. The show was titled: "How to Fight Well." Great title, so of course, I was locked in.

The guests for the episode were Jayson and Ellen Gladys, who own the Relationship School. They help couples create a healthy marriage that can lead their families to develop healthy relationships in their own lives.

The topic of arguing, of course, got brought up several times, and Ellen jumped in at one point and said something profound. I'll paraphrase...

When a couple argues, the process of how they heal together is more important than the actual healing. She went on to explain that showing up for one another and committing to improving the current situation is how couples demonstrate that they're on a team, working together to solve the same problem. When couples stop working together to solve their problems, that's when, experts say, the damage becomes worse.

Learning how to navigate problems and having a *process* for key decisions is critical to human development and the success of your business.

3 Magic Tools for Decision-Making

Decision-making is an art and a science. In my opinion, we should have something like a paint-by-numbers, which gives just enough creativity and just enough direction to optimize both flexibility and process.

Compiling a few pieces of decision-making criteria for your team will save you insane time, money, and energy. Early on, I would get frustrated with my team, because they kept asking me to make small purchases, like a $20 upgrade to a piece of software we needed.

These questions frustrated me to no end. *How can they not determine the answer to this on their own?* I thought. I wanted my team to understand what we were trying to accomplish and, yes, of course I'd approve $20 if that would make that happen. Instead of empowering my team to make their own enlightened decisions, I found myself constantly approving small purchases and splitting hairs over small things that didn't matter, like what images to use in decks and whether one text block came before another on one of our landing pages. It felt like the little decisions were zapping my decision-making energy.

One day I looked at my process around decisions. There wasn't one. I had general guidelines (which I'll explain here in a minute) that stemmed from our core values, but I never had the tactical elements my team needed to feel comfortable making their own decisions.

Now, I have 3 tools I offer them—an amount they're allowed to spend, questions to ask before they spend it, and one final question.

Tool 1: An Amount Each Can Spend

Everyone on your team should be able to answer this question: "How much am I allowed to spend to solve this problem?"

Basically, everyone on your team should have an amount they can spend to solve problems without needing to loop anyone else in. Usually, I ballpark this amount for my clients around $200-500 per employee, depending on your budget and your team structure.

It's incredible when you give your team the autonomy to solve problems and the guidance to get there. Things get solved. The people you have are typically pretty capable. It's actually you who gets in the way of most things. I found that to be true with my team. They'd come to me and ask for a piece of software, a course, to send a client a gift, and I'd go down the rabbit hole of helping them make the decision and solve the problem. Ultimately, it took longer to make the decision and, I'll admit again, at times, it frustrated me.

> **Every employee should know the answer:** "How much am I allowed to spend to solve this problem on my own?"

Now, everyone on my team understands their budget for solving problems and making decisions. They can ask peers for advice, but ultimately, they can make a cost decision (up to an amount) on their own. Today, I can focus on the decisions I absolutely must make.

There are tons of studies on decision fatigue. One from Harvard studied successful CEOs and their morning routines. It showed that some of the highest performing people in the word had the same morning routine for decades. Waking at the same time, eating the same breakfast, wearing the same outfit. We don't recognize the impact these little withdrawals have on our ability to make decisions in the war room, the ones that honestly matter for the trajectory of our firm.

As the founder or CEO, it's your responsibility to equip your team with the things they need to make these foundational decisions. Give them the tools they need, so you can protect your time, saving your energy for those instances where you need to be at your best, whether that's inking a new partnership, delivering a workshop to a group of perfect clients, developing a strategy for a new product or feature, or spending it on something else. Eliminate the small decisions from your desk.

Tool 2: Things to Keep in Mind When Making Decisions

I'm currently working with a client who provides medical care at correctional facilities. Over the years, I've worked in medical quite a bit, but when this interesting opportunity came across my desk, I was intrigued, and knew I had to help.

They explained to me in one of our very first meetings that the culture in jail is different than at a regular medical care facility. At a correctional facility, on-site decisions can make the difference between life and death, particularly if someone comes in and is in serious withdrawal from certain substances.

I helped my client develop some training for their staff, a vital tool for my client's employees to make quick, safe decisions.

Every decision tree will look different. Obviously, for my client's high-stakes work, we had a very targeted, niche set of information that informed his staff's decision-making. We took that information and trained them on exactly what they needed to keep in mind to make the best decisions in the moment of crisis.

At Operations Agency, I'm running a lower-stakes operation, so the information I give to my staff to help inform their decisions is very different. You'll need to make your own list of criteria for your specific operation, but I'll give you ours here at Operations Agency so you can get an idea of what this looks like:

A) Grow or Go

This one is one of my favorites. It's simple, and I use this to help me make some key decisions in my life and in my business. The simple filter is: will this help me grow? Whether it's in an activity that doesn't serve me, working with someone who is dragging me down, or deciding if a particular habit is a good or bad one. Everything flows through this decision-making filter of "grow or go."

In December 2022, Steve and I sat down to do an assessment of how we spend our time. We knew that we had some big goals coming up, and he was about to go back to school fulltime that upcoming January. We realized that we spent much of our down time vegging in front of the television after the kids went to bed. From about 8-9:30 pm each night we'd watch a handful of mindless episodes of *Modern Family* and then head to bed. Great show, but a huge time suck. We decided to take those 90 minutes back to grow instead. Now we read, he does his homework or writes papers for classes, or we simply enjoy each other's company. A huge life upgrade just from this one filter.

Always ask yourself: *Does this help me grow?* If not, it needs to go.

B) Treat People Like Family

I had a client once who had the meanest assistant ever—one of those people who was plain rude, wasn't a team player, and who took her power a little too seriously. Every time I contacted her, my energy drained. She made me realize that if we treat each other like members of our family, we'd probably get substantially further, faster. Here's the catch: We don't spend unlimited time with family. But when we do interact, we have a mutual respect that helps us move forward positively. I've implemented this with my team, and (maybe I'm biased), but they treat each other, me, and our clients amazingly well. They show up respectfully to meetings internally and externally and they're vulnerable and transparent in their communication. They don't want to let anyone down.

C) Will This Help Our Clients Win?

Client success will drive every other element of your work. If you obsess over helping your clients reach their own finish lines and improving their situation at every turn, you'll be lightyears ahead of your competition. Many companies, unfortunately, don't consider their customers as much as they should.

If you're just starting out, I have a simple formula for success:

- Find a handful of clients
- Obsess over their success
- Capture testimonials or case-studies from them
- Ask them to tell a few friends about you

If you do all the above, you'll be overloaded with work before you know it. There will probably be a waiting list to work with you.

If we filter our decisions by the best possible outcomes for our clients and customers, we'll create raving fans of our business.

D) Treat Company Money Like It's Your Own

This filter is simple: don't default to spending. Weigh the options first, then decide whether using financial resources is necessary. For some reason, folks have a hard time with other people's money. They either spend it too carefully or too recklessly. Treating it like it's your own is the best way I've found to crystallize to set the right tone. In fact, this rule has helped me in my personal life, as I've learned to invest more in my health and my family's quality time.

Those are just a few examples of some gentle guidelines you could add in place for your team to help them make decisions. These have saved my clients and me a ton of headaches. Depending on your industry, you may want to get more specific.

Tool 3: Up-to-Date & Accurate Data

I read an incredible book when I was pregnant with my first son called *Expecting Better* by Emily Oster. She's a data scientist turned parent advocate and has a handful of books about pregnancy and navigating parenting in a data-accessible way. If you're a parent, you know that most parenting advice comes with strings, or some kind of biased opinion layered over it.

Anyway, Oster's writing isn't like that. Her writing is clear, concise, and data-driven. As you'd probably expect from a data scientist, her approach to pregnancy was pragmatic and useful.

She broke the book down into the key decisions women need to make in their pregnancies (there are a great number of them) and placed studies and stories alongside those decisions to help the reader gather the data necessary to make the decisions they're comfortable with. Oster rarely states her own opinion or even her decisions with her own 2 pregnancies. She did do something, however, that I didn't expect, but it made me love the book even more.

She poked holes in the data she presented. She pointed out the flaws that many studies have, especially the smaller ones. I learned so much about data collection from reading this book that it made me question other things I held as "truths" just because there was a study conducted on the matter. Having the information you need to make good decisions is absolutely critical. (In some cases, the health and safety of your baby could be at stake.)

Much of the fear, anxiety, and reluctance that we feel around making decisions is really just a lack of clarity on the contextual information surrounding the decision.

If I get dressed in the morning or lay out my outfit the night before without looking at the weather for the next day, I've made a mistake (albeit a low stakes mistake). Without checking the weather I have no idea if I'm setting myself up to be uncomfortable all day long.

In pregnancy and in business, we're in the decision-making driver's seat. It's an unbelievable amount of pressure. Setting ourselves up with the information we need to make calm and quick decisions is going to be the difference between getting caught out in the rain with no jacket and pulling your mini-umbrella out of your bag. It's going to save us headaches and take the pain out of our operating functions.

Remember: we're on level 5, optimizing your business operations so that you make the best decisions possible.

Optimize Your Company Scorecard

When I was in high school, my friend Kara and I kept the basketball stats for one season, something I'd never done before (even though I'd always loved watching basketball). At a whopping 5 feet and 2 inches tall, with pretty terrible hand-eye coordination, I knew I'd never be a basketball player, but I could sure stay useful to the team from operating on the sidelines.

Armed with a green, spiral notebook and a list of players, numbers, positions, and a handful of other important data, Kara and I kept track. For every single game. It was not unusual to have 3 or 4 games in a week, depending on how well the team was performing.

Kara and I continue to document points, fouls, turnovers, rebounds, assists, free throws, and more.

The coaches, referees, and players used this data to decide who wasn't playing by the rules (too many fouls), who was scoring highest and performing their best, among other details. After each game, every coach would get a copy of the stats, which they would use to adjust their next practice to work on key areas of improvement.

It was epic. I loved keeping the stats. It was high-paced, interesting, and useful. Everyone had the exact information they needed to decide what to do next: how to run the next practice, or who to put in the next game. Decisions were no longer anxiety-inducing because everyone had the data they needed. Coaches in the pros use much of this data to recruit new players, negotiate terms of contracts, decide on playing time, and more, because much of it is publicly available.

Imagine if you had all the personal performance metrics for all your hires before you hired them? It'd be game-changing, and far less risky to invite them into your organization.

We can tap into this risk mitigation strategy and take advantage of using scoring methods in our own business with a company scorecard. You've probably already started yours in Chapter 6 when you started tracking your habits. Remember, the core areas we want to track are:

- #Marketing
- #Sales
- #Fulfillment
- #Product
- #Admin

You need to have at least one metric (but maybe more) per area. You also need to determine who owns which metric. Then, you need to set the following standards for those metrics.

I love my scorecard metrics to have a few other things defined, as well:

1. **What is the metric?**
   Be as specific as possible; we don't want this to get convoluted and all of a sudden, we're looking at faulty data. Simple is good, too. Example: "How much time does it take us to onboard a new client?"

2. **What is the source of truth?**
   Where do we look to find this information? Is it accurate, or might we need to do a little calculating to arrive at the final number that should be added to the scorecard?

3. **Who is the owner?**
   I can't tell you how many times I've worked with teams who are collecting data for a specific metric, but since there's no owner of that metric, it never gets looked at, discussed, or updated. Make sure every important metric has an owner responsible for it. That individual should update it on the scorecard, and they (or someone else) should be responsible for improving the metric.

4. **What is the goal, and what are the acceptable ranges?**
   Remember our traffic light system from earlier? Use that here, too. When we build scorecards for our clients, we define the acceptable ranges of the metric to make sure to flag under- and over- performance. Where do we pivot? Where do we double down?

5. **What is the cadence for review?**

We may look at some metrics weekly and others daily. We may decide that monthly is the best time to look at all our metrics together to make key decisions. Whatever the situation is for you and your company, make sure the scorecard is being filled out and those meetings for review are scheduled in advance. If everything is going well, those meetings should only take 10-15 minutes.

A Note on Team Management

Let's talk about team management here for a quick second.

In my experience, Scorecards are a slightly heavy lift because most of this may be brand new to the team. And the roll-out is going to be tricky. We want to establish buy-in with our team and help them understand that, ultimately, this will help everyone communicate more effectively and be able to support one another more openly. Being transparent about goals opens us up to receive more help, coaching, and resources.

Imagine a player on the basketball team I managed was consistently struggling with high turnover. I bet you can guess the topic of conversation between him and the coach at their next practice. Or imagine that someone was missing free throws left and right? The coach can determine that, because they can compare the stats—within those documents, everything's right there, the solutions, the next steps, the areas of improvement, all open for all to see.

The practice of having a company Scorecard has not only helped me grow my team members' skills and my business, but it's also helped me have tough conversations around performance.

When we have centralized company data, there's not a ton of ambiguity around who is pulling their weight and who isn't. Thankfully, I have a rockstar team at Operations Agency. When we review the Scorecard each week, I see the highs and lows. Most of the time, my team comes to the table telling *me* why the Scorecard looks the way it does, then, they provide their best solutions to get back on track by the end of the week.

This single scorecard is a fantastic tool that has significantly decreased the amount of performance conversations I must have with my growing team of 14 employees and contractors. Instead of blind-siding someone with a quarterly or end-of-year performance review, they can make smaller adjustments throughout the year with the scorecard.

Centralizing the company's data in a highly visible scorecard may feel pretty vulnerable at first, for you and the whole team, but there are a few reasons why centralizing the data in front of the entire team is helpful.

First of all, no one is better than anyone else, and no one is above these metrics. You need metrics, too, as the owner, to show your team that you also hold responsibility for your performance, consistency, and how you show up to your work. This needs to be a shared effort by everyone on the team. I'm not asking your assistant to fill everything out and present it to the team. Everyone must jump in and fill out their portion of the metrics.

When my husband joined the military, he went through basic training, just like everyone else. It was rigorous, all-consuming, and lasted for 3 months. He ate, bathed, slept (or mostly didn't), and did basically everything in between with the people in his platoon. The people he was with were from all walks of life. They were also from all corners of the United States, and some, who wanted to serve in our military to gain legal citizenship, were even from different countries. The personality differences were vast, but the outcomes for training were clear: do the task at hand as quickly or for as long as you can.

There are various opinions about the purpose of basic training in the military. Some say that its purpose is to strip you of your identity and ensure that you'll be an obedient soldier. My opinion is that the core purpose of basic training is to give you shared experiences so that you're willing to do whatever you have to do to support the person standing next to you. Shared experiences are the ultimate comradery builders. Plus, everyone's performance is out in the open, and everyone gets punished or rewarded based on group behavior. You're only as strong as your weakest link.

I'm not suggesting that we all gather our teammates in the conference room and make them do pushups for 45 minutes straight, but you get the idea. Centralizing performance metrics will incentivize the team to show up differently because they don't want to let the team down. And those folks who are putting up amazing numbers will be able to lead those who are struggling and encourage them to rise to meet their goals.

The Scorecard breeds leaders. Looking at the metrics every week, you can clearly see who has the tools to succeed, who is showing up consistently, and who is taking their metrics seriously. Typically, when your company reaches over $1 million in revenue, you should focus on creating leaders and a feedback loop for those leaders. The Scorecard creates both.

3 Operational Functions: People, Process, & Systems

There are 3 things to consider when reading your scorecard: people, process, and systems. They typically flow together to create the outcomes we seek in our business.

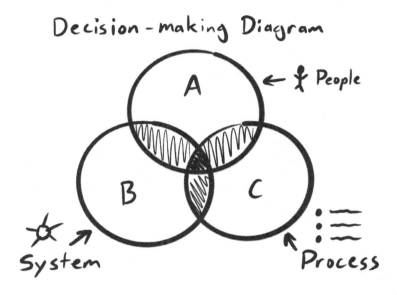

We want to keep this in mind when reading our Scorecard, almost as a filter to discover how things are going.

I worked with a client once who wanted to track a metric of less than one error per week. So, to be clear, he wanted zero errors.

His metric made me think about that episode of *The Office* where an offbeat, but generally stellar sales performer, Dwight Schrute, is fed up with his colleagues' performance, so he creates this doomsday device. The rules were that if anyone makes a mistake, even a simple calculation error, it would count as a strike. The entire team only got 5 strikes in a one-day period. The stick? If they reached 5 strikes, the system would automatically email their CEO, Jo Bennet, with all the nasty emails the team had written about her since she'd taken the helm.

Dwight had created an intricate system to track these errors and it could only be accessed by password that he withheld from the rest of the team. For the viewer, the scenario is comical. If this happened on an actual workday, it'd be terrifying.

Back to my client.

He had this lofty expectation of zero errors, but no way to track this. So, he wanted to look at a zero-errors goal in each of his departments, but they didn't have the systems to review real data about performance.

So, I asked him:

"What do you track that would help you understand that no errors are happening, or more accurately, that even if there are errors happening, you're still meeting quality and efficiency metrics?"

He said his project management tool, Jira, would be a great place to begin.

When I got in there, it was a mess. There was no consistency, it looked like projects hadn't been updated anytime recently. It was impossible to gather any data that was meaningful enough to have a conversation about it. I showed him our ops functions Venn diagram and explained that for a metric to function well, we need to support our people with a clear process and a system to be able to perform with zero errors.

We worked together to create a consistent project management system that tracked outcomes and timeline only, which helped the team get their head around their expectations and offered them an easy feedback loop. Not only was my client happy with the results and the new (shorter) turnaround time on projects and tasks, but the team was also helping co-create solutions for Jira. They were creating automation to save even more time, holding meetings with other team members to help them build similar functions. It was really cool to see. The team's leadership skills and productivity were laying right under the surface that entire time.

We often think we need to do more to manage our team in order to get results. As my client thought when we first began, we often think we need to focus on "making zero mistakes." A slight shift in the opposite direction, a quick focus on what we *do* want instead of what we *don't* want can make all the difference.

Whenever we see a metric that's underperforming or perhaps isn't completely clear, take a look at the 3 operational functions and ask yourself a few questions.

1. Do I have a consistent **process** created and documented to generate the desired results?
2. Do I have a **system** to look at as a source of truth?
3. Do I have a **person** dedicated to this metric and the process, and does this person have the tools and training necessary to achieve the desired outcome?

After we've created the baseline foundation for how we operate, using the scorecard with the critical elements on it will tell us where to focus our time and resources. When we establish our goals at the beginning of each quarter, reviewing them with our team, and asking those critical questions above will help you and your team make decisions around updating core processes, managing and implementing new technology, and even making key new hires. If you have a team member who's in charge of multiple metrics, and one or 2 start to slip, this is a good time to have a conversation to see if you need to hire someone else because their role has expanded.

The Scorecard and a healthy feedback loop (usually in team huddles and one-on-one employee meetings) will give you the status report you and your leadership team need to make informed decisions, quickly. And it unites the team under one shared goal we can easily wrap our arms around.

A few years ago, my parents bought a bar in my hometown of West Deptford, New Jersey. They had their first full day of ownership on March 10, 2020. Five days later, restaurants and bars all over the world closed their doors and wondered if they'd ever open them again. They were met with immediate resistance and some major challenges from opening up an outdoor area and installing shower curtains between seats at the counter, but they managed to stay open, and now, they're thriving.

My dad probably has one of the biggest hearts of anyone I know. He's always doing things for others and very rarely for himself. He also has a little motto he taught me when I was younger and reluctant to empty our dishwasher.

"If you're not going to do it right, don't bother doing it at all."

This phrase has helped shape my standards of excellence into adulthood and, I think, contributes to my overall success in so many ways. But just like my dad, I can take it too far, getting caught up in the details.

If we're not careful, the "do it right" mantra can lead us to split hairs over small things in our businesses, like what kind of fonts to use or what kind of lettuce to put on the burger special that week. Splitting hairs on details is great—for the right decisions. For the wrong ones, it can cripple our growth and even hold us back from ever fully delegating anything.

Decisions will rule our day-to-day if we don't get a handle on how they are presented to us. We need to grab the wheel of our business, determine what the most important numbers are (both leading and lagging), and review those consistently to make decisions that will have statistically favorable outcomes. We don't need to see everything; we need to see the right things.

Yours operationally.

Summary:

- Making powerful decisions allows you to shape your life and your business.

- Making the right decisions brings you ultimate impact.

- Place specific metrics in front of specific team members to shape their decision-making abilities.

- Give your team (and yourself) a set of guidelines to keep things objective.

Critical Action:

Create decision making guidelines for you and your team. Remember to include the metrics that will help to inform those decisions.

CHAPTER 10

PUTTING IT ALL TOGETHER

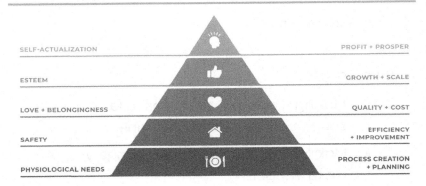

> **Mission:** It's time to take action. Because you've already waited too long.

Remember Miranda from the beginning of our journey together, the business owner who came down with a sudden illness and was forced to stop working in her business? Although her sabbatical was forced, focusing on the 5 key levels helped her tremendously and gave her peace of mind that things were not going to fall apart in her absence. We worked with her Chief of Staff to make sure that there were systems in place for what was going well and created new opportunities for her coaching community to refer and generate new business for them. The model we created for Miranda during her Sabbatical can, and likely will, be the foundation that takes her coaching business to the next level. Allowing Miranda and her coaching teams to land government contracts and coach at a higher capacity.

This reset, this pullback, was an opportunity. And although Miranda was really going through some hard challenges, her positivity and passion was inspiring. She knew it was all happening at the exact right moment, and her experience would serve her—and her clients—long term.

In nature, every single being needs rest. Plants literally grow while resting, not while gathering sunlight and nutrients. The way that nature can thrive independent of any one being is because it exists in an ecosystem designed to get specific outcomes. Let your business operations determine your ecosystem so that you can rest and grow.

My hope for you, is that you won't wait until something breaks, or until someone quits, or until your health is in shambles, or until your family is about to fall apart. Don't wait.

Each rest point is a micro-deposit into a long-term vision of success. You want your muscles to repair, you want to gain fresh perspective, you want to breed leaders and have a business that can function like an ecosystem: to act as the sum of its parts.

Use your sabbatical to empower team members to create solutions to problems, place your trust in your systems and write them down, plan goals and initiatives that can stabilize you through high-growth periods. It's not sexy, and it's often not fun. But it works. It's worked for a great deal of my clients and it can work for you if you commit and own your habits as an owner.

There probably wouldn't be a Bill and Melinda Gates foundation without Gates' famous Sabbatical in 1999. Imagine if Bill

Gates had burnt out like my client Miranda and was too over-whelmed to launch his anti-malaria program, which prevented 1.7 billion cases of malaria and saved 10.6 million lives. [16]

Gates now consistently implements mini-sabbaticals of one-week, where he pauses his life, goes off-grid, and thinks. He literally calls each of these 7-day periods a "Think Week."

Another incredible example of some remote-control management is Yvon Chouinard, founder of Patagonia.

In the 1980s, Patagonia was growing rapidly, and Chouinard realized that he was no longer able to manage all aspects of the business on his own. He stepped back from daily operations and focused on his passion for outdoor sports and environmental activism.

Chouinard appointed a new CEO, Kris McDivitt[17], to lead the company's day-to-day operations. McDivitt had been working at Patagonia for several years and had a strong background in retail and operations management. Chouinard remained involved in the company as the chairman of the board and continued to shape its vision and values. He also used his platform to promote environmental causes and encourage sustainable business practices.

Under McDivitt's leadership, Patagonia continued to grow and expand while staying true to its core values of environmentalism and social responsibility. The company became a leader in sustainable business practices, implementing initiatives such as the Common Threads Partnership, which encouraged customers to repair and reuse their Patagonia products rather than buying new ones.

---

[16] https://www.gatesfoundation.org/our-work/programs/global-health/malaria

[17] At the time, she was *Kris Tompkins*

The decision to remove Chouinard from the daily operations of Patagonia allowed the company to continue growing while maintaining its core values and principles. Chouinard could now focus on his passions and use his platform to promote environmental causes.

In an interview with *Inc. Magazine,* the writer asked McDivitt if Chouinard's absences affect morale, She sorely replied:

"Are you saying he's not working because he's not here sitting at a desk beating the shit out of people? When Yvon's gone, he's working. He's got product with him, and he always comes home with new ideas. That question drives me nuts."

Her boss's global trekking has resulted in reforestation projects in Chile, relationship-cementing ski trips with dealers in Japan, and chance encounters with mountain climbers offering valuable feedback on equipment. "Do you know what all that's worth? It's like gold," she said in the *Inc.* interview. "It's all about how you form relationships with people."

Now, Patagonia offers these benefits to all employees with their groundbreaking sabbatical policy. They've recognized that their company can thrive if it holds true to why it exists, creates quality products and experience for customers, and can operate independently of any one person on the team.

Including the founder.

A Note on Maintenance

When we moved to the south in 2017, it was a huge change in lifestyle and pace. Steve and I grew up in the bustling northeast and hadn't spent much time outside of New Jersey, New York, and Philadelphia.

Moving to a small, military town outside of Nashville, Tennessee presented its challenges and opportunities.

As we settled into the area, I would frequently get frustrated with the generally longer turnaround times with services, the calm pace in which the clerk at Publix scanned my grocery items, and the fact that full-service coffee shops (outside of Starbucks) simply didn't exist.

I did what most northeastern folks did—I judged. I assumed "slow" meant "lacking education," lacking drive," or "lacking grit."

That could not have been further from the truth.

Interestingly, after getting to know several people in the area, I realized that the reason that things operated slower down south wasn't because of a *lacking* of anything. It was simply because their baseline knowledge for maintaining what they had was much greater than what I'd experienced up north.

At first glance, I wondered why there was only one plumber, one fence company, one nail salon. It was frustrating to me that these folks had very little competition, something I was convinced was the reason for slow service.

However, overall, the *need* for services in this area was lower. You rarely heard, "There's a leak. Call the plumber." Why? Because people in this small town just generally fixed the leak themselves.

It's challenging to be confronted with your own bigotry, but there we were, in a state that we now called home, and we were learning that the reason these folks could be calm was because they had their baseline needs figured out. They could fix their own leaks, change their own oil, build their own barns, grow their own food, and, in some cases, live completely sustainably.

They were much less dependent on the external. They had what they needed, and they could maintain those needs without relying on anyone. It was calming. Finally, I understood why the pace felt slower.

Maintenance is a traditionally unsexy word. We think of someone in coveralls approaching our car holding a random wrench. It's tedious, it takes us away from the other things we need or want to be doing. My note here on maintenance for your business (and life): make things simple enough that you can maintain most items on your own.

In my experience, companies who overcomplicate their operations end up tossing out most of what they have because it simply becomes too much to maintain. The team doesn't buy-in and then you may end up in a worse spot than where you started.

John Deere is a company that has been manufacturing tractors since the 1830s. Over the years, they have become known for producing reliable, high-quality tractors capable of performing a wide range of agricultural tasks. John Deere tractors generally require regular upkeep to keep them running smoothly. This includes tasks such as changing the oil and filters, checking, and adjusting the tire pressure, and lubricating moving parts.

The specific maintenance requirements for a John Deere tractor will depend on the model and year of manufacture. However, some general guidelines that apply to most models include:

1. Changing the oil and oil filter every 100 hours of operation or once per year, whichever comes first.
2. Checking the air filter every 50 hours of operation and replacing it as needed.
3. Checking and adjusting the tire pressure regularly to ensure even wear and proper traction.

4. Lubricating all moving parts, including the engine, transmission, and steering system.

5. Checking the battery and charging system regularly to ensure proper function.

6. Inspecting and replacing worn or damaged belts and hoses.

7. Checking and adjusting the brakes, clutch, and other systems as needed.

This is a pretty reasonable list of maintenance items. However, one of the ways that John Deere has cemented its hold on the marketplace is by requiring that their tractors be maintained by certified maintainers if they want to keep their warranties valid. This method of a company monopolizing the maintenance on expensive products it sells isn't a new practice by any means (Kodak did the same thing back in the 1990s). Still, the Department of Justice is investigating whether these practices are, in fact, legal. John Deere owns 53 percent of the market share for tractors in the United States, and when one of their tractors require repairs beyond regular maintenance, farmers have reported that going through certified maintainers can put their tractors out of commission for months at a time. A few months off for a farmer could put them at risk of wasting an entire season's worth of harvest.

The lawsuit from Forest River Farms has encouraged the Federal Trade Commission to create right-to-repair policies to protect farmers from having their warranties voided should they decide to maintain their own equipment.

My point is—even farmers know that there's a sincere cost to being beholden to a specific party, waiting on their timeline to get back to business as usual. Your business is just like the farmer's farm—it can't wait on you to be "available" as the certified maintainer.

The ability to maintain your own operations to an extent is a critical factor for your success. You want to have a basic understanding of how things work and be able to have the ability to make tweaks where necessary as you go. But you also want to equip your farm and its workers to maintain the equipment themselves.

One Last Thing. . .

By now you understand how to create a sustainable business, how to use rest strategically, and how to remove yourself from the day-to-day operations of your business. There's a lot of benefit to defining how you operate, implementing consistent ways to measure outcomes, and allowing those to help you and your team make decisions long term.

Just like anything in life worth doing, operations is a practice. A discipline. And, unfortunately, too many owners are too proud to admit their own limitations, so they crumble. Don't be those people. I've never been in a situation where relying on tested and true methods didn't work. Eating whole foods, getting great sleep, not drinking alcohol, increasing my water intake are all basics that have contributed to my physical wellbeing. Creating processes and defining clear outcomes, quality measurables, and decision-making guidelines, are the basics for a healthy business. Establish this baseline, lay the foundation, and use it to catapult your business into the next best fun thing where you can try new ideas, test boundaries, reach to change the world and improve life for its inhabitants. But we need to cover the basics, and make sure we have a system to assess and improve them.

In the early 1950s, experts believed that it was impossible for a human being to run a mile in under 4 minutes. However, Roger Bannister, a medical student at the time, was determined to break the barrier. He developed a simple training regimen that consisted of running intervals and hill sprints, and he would train for 30 minutes a day, often fitting in his workouts between classes.

On May 6, 1954, Bannister made history by running a mile in 3 minutes and 59.4 seconds. His simple training regimen had produced a high outcome, and his accomplishment inspired countless others to push their own limits.

Bannister didn't rely on any fancy equipment or cutting-edge training methods. Instead, he focused on consistency, discipline, and outcomes (his mile time), proving that simple approaches can push even the human body outside its preconceived limits.

Like Kobe Bryant said, "The best never get bored with the basics."

Bannister's training program included 10 x 440-meter repeats with 2 minutes rest between. He focused on consistency, on tracking his improvements on his split, what he put into his body, and his rest. He didn't overcomplicate his training, he didn't attempt to reinvent the wheel.; he simply invested time and energy into what he knew worked.

Actualizing your dreams takes courage and a willingness to do hard things that others won't. I'm not going to tell you it will be easy. Being a high-performer and achieving great things in life and in business includes sacrifice. My encouragement to you is this: sacrifice the right things. Sacrifice working late, doing things you don't love. Sacrifice *missing* your kids' sports games. Sacrifice another argument with your spouse about how much time you spend away from home. Sacrifice the things that you know, deep down, aren't serving you. Television, alcohol, junk food, social media. . . these are all vices that we make time for that don't serve us. Make time for the essentials. Move your body, drink water, play with your kids, hug your spouse, go see a friend, level up your skills, read a book. And, for heaven's sake, take a rest.

I believe in you. I support you. You've got this.

Yours operationally,

Alyson

WHAT'S NEXT?

Here you are. About to close this journey together and get that little dopamine hit you get when you finish something. Now that you understand how to use rest strategically to grow your business and bring a little more peace to your life, it's time to implement what you've learned.

So many folks will get an injection of excitement around getting started and then they forget that they need to stick with it. The true test of whether you're ready to implement the Sabbatical Method into your lifestyle will come when you put down this book. What will you do next?

First, if you have not gone through and completed all the Critical Actions, do that now. I designed this book to make sure as your business grows and life changes, you can flip back through the chapters, read the summaries, and use the toolkit to complete your Critical Actions.

Second, go grab the toolkit with all the lessons, video walkthroughs, worksheets, and a ton of templates over at thesabbaticalmethod.com/toolkit.

Third, connect with me if you want some support. At Operations Agency, we support owners in getting their business out of their brain and down onto paper. It's brought so much clarity and calm to the folks we've worked with. I know it can change your business, too. If you want to work with us to create processes on-demand, head over to operationsagency.com to learn more.

Finally, if you're unsure where to begin or what the next step is for you, start small. If some of what we discussed is challenging and you're rethinking your entire existence, know that wasn't my goal but that has been something that I've personally gone through. It'll be OK. You'll figure it out. Start with small wins, and incremental progress. It will build back to big momentum in no time.

My hope for you is that you develop sustainability and longevity, that you create a life that you love living every day, not just at the high moments. I want you to have a business that is flourishing without ruling your life.

At the end of the day, operations = outcomes. Reverse engineer how you need to live your life and run your business to achieve the outcomes you want. But always remember that outcomes $\neq$ happiness. Happiness happens on the path, in the day-to-day. It doesn't wait for us to arrive. We're already here. Let's find joy in what we have today and a plan for the rest.

ACKNOWLEDGEMENTS

Without the love and support of my family and the team at Operations Agency, this book would not have been possible. To Steve who inspires me every day to be the best version of myself. I'm certain I'll keep learning and growing alongside you for the rest of my life. To my 2 boys, Frank and Jack, for teaching me that life is abundant, and time is precious. Becoming your mother has challenged and enlightened me in countless ways, I am simply a better person after having you both. There is so much to come, and I'm honored to be one of your guides. To my parents, Denice and John, 2 incredible role models and an unwavering support system. Mom, by believing in me you taught me to believe in myself. A skill that I will cherish always. Dad, you said 'if you're not going to do it right, don't do it at all.' You've woven a standard of excellence into my blood that has been a driving force behind my work and the impact I hope to make. Life is sweeter because you guys are the champions of our dreams. I love you both very much.

To Cody and Christy Burch, 2 amazing friends, colleagues, and human beings. Your encouragement and friendship have meant so much to me over the years of running my business and growing my family. To Madison Moore, my incredible first hire at Operations Agency and one of the professionals I feel has understood my vision the most in my career thus far. You've been cheering this book on since its inception and I am so grateful to finally deliver. I'll always cherish the time that you spent collaborating and creating amazing things with me. I can't wait to see you become a mom of your own. To Kelly Kannett, my hype woman and the person I can be completely and totally myself around. Everyone deserves a person in their life like you. You are magnetic and powerful and I'm happiest when you are near. To Marcel Petitpas, a friend and a coach. You probably don't even know this, but you pulled me out of a funk last year and called me to action. You're incredibly intelligent and wildly compassionate. Your whole heart is dedicated to serving and I thank you for everything you've poured into my business over the years. To my wonderful right-hand-gal, Lauren Cottam. I can't imagine what Operations Agency would be like today without your patience and practical solutions for our team and our clients. You really are the glue that holds everything together. The Yin to my Yang. Thank you for giving me the time and space to be able to focus on the things that light me up. Your presence at work is calming, you are an inspiring mother and an all-around wonderful person.

For all my people, personal and professional, who stood by me with patience and grace over the last few years while I navigated all the messy changes of life, new motherhood, business ownership, and all my roles, I see you and I appreciate you.

To all my wonderful clients past and present at Operations Agency for showing up, trusting me, and committing to operating better, I honor you.

To the editing, publishing, visuals, and marketing teams. Paul Fair, Timmy Bauer, Allie Tymozco, Kerk Murray and the team, and SelfPublishing.com. Wow. I tapped you all on the shoulder and had a crazy idea to launch and promote this book. You all sprung to action and supported me entirely. Without hesitation. The guidance, the support, and the answers to millions of questions mean the world to me. You all handled everything with precision so that I could simply create the words on the page. Paul, for making my writing more elegant and helping me crystallize a lot of ideas. Timmy, for being willing to go above and beyond on the print timeline and laying out my pages. Allie, for creating a look and feel that allows readers and people who experience our brand to feel safe, supported, and cared for. Kerk, for giving me the action items to amplify my message and make sure folks hear about this lifesaving method.

To Dan Martell, who gave me an opportunity to be a partner in his community and created a space to confront a lot of my feelings of unworthiness and doubt. I literally became a different person after coming to one of your events and I thank you for showing up the way you do. It's inspiring.

Finally, thank *you* for caring. Thank you for the difference you are making with your products and your services. Picking up this book, reading it to completion, and implementing its actions are going to change the way you work and live. I am certain. Thank you for believing in yourself, for trusting me as your guide, and for your commitment to improving your business operations.

ABOUT THE AUTHOR

Alyson Caffrey is best known for her ability to optimize backend operations so that Founders can create an asset that operates independently of them.

She is a small-business Operations Strategist and a sought-after fractional COO for:

- Thought leaders

- *Inc.* 5000 Companies

- High-growth digital agencies

- Founders who want to run a business that lasts

She is also a wife, a mom of 2 little boys, loves yard work, and devours books about business.

Made in the USA
Middletown, DE
30 May 2023

31481122R00116